What to Expect: A Mom's Perspective

EATING DISORDER RECOVERY

A Simplified Guide for Families

CAROLINE R. BLAIRE

This book contains advice and information related to healthcare. It is not intended to replace medical advice and should be used to supplement rather than replace regular care by your doctor. It is recommended that you seek your physician's advice before embarking on any health plan. All efforts have been made to assure the accuracy of the information contained in this book as of the date of publication.

The publisher and the author disclaim any liability for any medical outcomes that may occur as a result of applying the methods suggested in this book. In order to ensure privacy and protection to people mentioned throughout this book, some names have been changed. It is the author's firm wish to respect her daughters' rights to share their respective stories with whom and when they choose.

Published by **Blaire Books**

Copyright © 2017 by Caroline R. Blaire

Print ISBN: 978-0692868096

All rights reserved. No portion of this book may be reproduced mechanically, electronically, or by any other means, including photocopying, without written permission of the publisher. It is illegal to copy this book, post it to a website, or distribute it by any other means without permission from the publisher.

Cover art by Amelia Blaire
Cover and interior layout by Gary A. Rosenberg

Printed in the United States of America

About the Cover Art

My younger daughter, Amelia, painted the art work featured on the cover of this book. Amelia finds art (both visual and performing art), not only her favorite activity, but also a highly effective coping strategy. Painting calms and distracts her from her negative body image, while singing fills her spirit with joy and happiness. At the time she painted this piece, Amelia was just thirteen years old, and through painting she had already begun to independently devise and implement her own recovery strategies. She used an abundance of periwinkle in this work, which unbeknownst to her at the time, is the color used for the symbol of the National Association of Anorexia Nervosa and Associated Disorders (ANAD) to represent and bring awareness of eating disorders.

*For my family—
my two lovely daughters
and loving husband, Joe.*

Contents

Acknowledgments ix

Author's Note xi

Introduction:
Could This Be an Eating Disorder? 1

PART I
What We Now Know About Eating Disorders

1. Important Concepts 17

2. Eating Disorder Basics 27

3. Why Is This Happening? 41

4. The Enigmatic Aspects of a Mysterious Disease 53

5. Getting Clear on Distorted Body Image 69

6. The Eating Disordered Mind and Change in Personality 75

PART II
Getting Help, Navigating Roadblocks, and Facilitating Recovery

7. How to Talk About Treatment   83
8. Treatment Options   91
9. Practice, Practice, Practice   105
10. A Unified Approach   111
11. Facilitating Strategies   117

References   125

About the Author   131

Acknowledgments

While this book was written to share my journey, writing it has been an adventure all its own. Without the strength and willingness of my brave and dedicated daughters, this book would not exist. Jillian and Amelia, I admire your dedication to your recoveries. As we celebrate our many blessings each and every day, including your recoveries, know this is all part of a greater journey, and I am eternally grateful to have been part of it. I love you both with all my heart.

To the most fun-loving, doting, involved, well-meaning, and compassionate husband and father. None of us is perfect, but you come pretty-darn close. You were my rock during the most challenging time in our lives. Your encouragement throughout this endeavor kept me going. You are, and will forever be, my best friend and soul mate. I love you.

I deeply appreciate the assistance and honest feedback during the early drafts from my father-in-law, Joe Sr., and

Mr. Tim Grandy. I am grateful to my mother, who as always, was there for us in countless ways.

Thank you to Jenni Schaefer, author of numerous titles on the topic of eating disorders, including *Life Without Ed*, Tracey Cornella-Carlson, M.D., who at the time of my daughters' illnesses served as Medical Director of the Child and Adolescent Eating Disorder Services at Rogers Memorial Hospital and continues to serve as Medical Director of the REDI Clinic in Milwaukee, as well as Lauren Mulheim, Psy.D., expert contributor for verywell.com (formerly called About.com), and Clinical Director of the Eating Disorder Informational website, Mirror-Mirror Eating Disorders. These experts kindly read, consulted, and assisted me in my effort to provide the most current, accurate, and insightful information. They offered me meaningful words of encouragement and, where needed, directed me to the works of other leading experts. I've learned some valuable information, not only during our journey toward recovery, but also in the process of writing this book. Thank you to Gary Rosenberg of The Book Couple, who designed the interior and cover of the book, bringing my daughter's art to life, and helped me with all stages of the publishing process. Finally, I wish to thank Michele Matrisciani for her publishing expertise and editorial skillfulness in helping me transform my work and prepare this book for publication.

Author's Note

I have two daughters, and both suffered with eating disorders, specifically anorexia nervosa. If you are reading this, it is most likely because you love someone who is confronting an eating disorder, or at least you suspect it based on his or her atypical behavior or expression of signs or symptoms. There is a time when we as caregivers may wonder if this really could be an eating disorder, and then we excuse, deny, or justify the worrisome behavior. I certainly did. If you are unsure, follow your intuition, let your instincts guide you, and seek professional help. During my daughters' simultaneous treatments and recoveries, I needed to learn a great deal about eating disorders, the recovery process, and my role in supporting my daughters in their difficult times. There are many valuable books out there, and I bought some of them, but every moment of my day and night was filled with concern, which made it impossible for me to focus on reading. The conversations between my husband, Joe, and myself were preoccupied by our daughters' eating disorders, treatment, and how we would endure it all. I just couldn't drum up the physical, emotional, and mental energy to research and learn when I was exhausted. Most books appeared too complicated, felt scholarly and academic, or were personal memoirs. Because I was already consumed with eating disorders twenty-four hours a day, seven days a week, most books lay at my bedside, never to be cracked open. There are many terrific resources available for families of those suffering eating disorders, and this book has not been written to be read in lieu of them but as a supplemental guide. I strongly encourage you to read the resources available, and learn to arm yourself with information. My intention is to offer you a simpler version of what's out there that highlights important aspects of assisting recovery while offering hope from someone who has been in the trenches, exactly where you find yourself now—times two!

During this exasperating time, I found healthcare professionals, including psychiatrists, therapists, nurses, and dieticians, especially helpful. Our family sessions were informative, instructional, and illuminating, and my husband and I were able to learn about our daughters' illnesses and recoveries. It was with these special people that we were able to unload concerns and seek answers and clarification to our questions.

The wealth of my current knowledge did not come overnight but came from witnessing my daughters tackle their problems both in treatment and at home and successfully navigate their respective recoveries.

Author's Note

I am not an expert. I am not a professional with specialized training in eating disorders. What I am is a mother with, what I believe to be, a good sense of what information you may be immediately in need of. I can remember which facts, advice, and research had the biggest impact on helping my husband and me. During our steep learning curve, we came across information that was downright confusing or abstract. Now with the benefit of time, clarity, perspective, investigation, and consultation with experts and other family advocates, I feel confident that I can boil down much of it here to help you *right now*.

Although my experience was specifically with anorexia nervosa and the coexisting problems of obsessive-compulsive disorder, anxiety, and depression, I believe much of the information I have uncovered applies to all eating disorders. It is my hope that by sharing this information in a simplified guide, families can become a better source of support in assisting their loved ones through recovery with the best outcomes possible.

Additionally, I have learned a great deal since my daughters have recovered, profoundly important and insightful information that I wish I had had when they were sick. Had I known then what I know now, I am certain I would have been less frustrated and much more patient and compassionate.

I fully appreciate your need for information and brevity. Think of this as your "What to Expect" guide, offering you key aspects and topics I regard as being most relevant to my own experiences. Essentially, I have written the book

I believe my husband and I would have benefited from years ago.

It is my sincere hope that within this book, you will begin to gain information on how to prepare yourself for supporting your loved one toward a successful recovery, one that results in personal growth, self-awareness, and stronger family bonds.

INTRODUCTION

Could This Be an Eating Disorder?

I begged my older daughter, at the time a freshman in high school, to tell me *please, why aren't you eating? What's going on?* But I already knew the answers. She just was unable to say the words.

And I wasn't ready to hear them.

Then, I ignored the signs in my younger daughter who was barely a teenager, and two years younger than her sister. Her hair began to fall out and she would gather it up from the bathroom floor and put it on the vanity for me to see—a silent cry for help. I'd clean it up, and she'd do it again, and I'd clean it up again, but I could not bring myself to speak about it. I wasn't ready to give into the realities of my daughters' suffering because to me that meant letting go of our lives and identities as we knew them.

What happened to my life? Our lives? When I let myself begin to think about my daughters' behaviors and symptoms, there was a sense of loss: a realization that life as I knew it would never be the same and that our futures would be forever altered—and not for the better. My mind went directly to the worst-case scenarios I had heard about, fixating on the people I knew who were unable to live happy, fulfilling lives, and those who lost their lives to anorexia. So, to push those fears away, I convinced myself and my husband that our daughters had anything but eating disorders.

If you have found this book, perhaps it is because you suspect your loved one has an eating disorder. Commend yourself for getting this far. The last thing you want to do is justify the behavior as a phase, willpower, or rebellion, and bury your head in the sand like I did in the beginning. Go with your gut, listen to your intuition, and be led by your instincts. If you are asking yourself, *could this be an eating disorder?* chances are you have cause for concern. Find a professional—a medical doctor, therapist, nurse practitioner, psychologist, anyone—and ask whether this could be an illness that requires immediate attention.

For fear that I would call attention to a "phase," only to exacerbate it into an actual problem, I talked myself into believing my husband and I could handle it. *It'll get better; she'll grow out of it.* I was afraid of facing the issue as a real illness because doing so would disrupt our lives in ways that I did not feel prepared for. As my daughters grew thinner and more sickly looking, I believe I went into shock, and my response was to further ignore it and not admit that it was a real problem. I thought, *this just isn't happening. If I ignore it, maybe it will just go away.*

What actually made matters worse was deciding to

keep my concerns to myself and not share them with other important, trusted, and supportive people in my life. I feared that if I spoke of it, I would make it real. I felt that the eating disorder(s) was a reflection of me and the things I've done wrong as a mother. It *had* to be my fault. The shame I lived with made everything worse. I kept going along as if nothing were wrong, all the while plagued by this dark secret perpetuating in my soul. Then there was the fear of judgment from others, which is what made me begin to hide in protection of myself, my family, and, most of all, my daughters. I knew others would become suspicious just by the looks of my girls, and I certainly did not want to hear their comments, which would only validate what I didn't want to face. I worried about the unusual behaviors and family dynamics around mealtime, so I backed away from social activities that included food, and, after a short time, disengaged completely. I made excuses for the way my daughters looked—weak and sunken. I told people things like, *oh, she's really stressed lately and hasn't been sleeping well.*

I employed any explanation to mitigate my own suspicion that my daughters had eating disorders. But guess what? All this denial didn't change the fact that my daughters had real problems and needed real help.

An eating disorder is an illness and must be taken seriously. It can even become life threatening. The longer a person has an eating disorder without seeking professional help, the longer the eating disorder behaviors are being practiced. The longer the behaviors are practiced, the better your loved one becomes at doing them, and the more difficult the behaviors may be to extinguish, and the greater the likelihood that over time additional eating disorder behaviors will develop.

For those intentionally attempting to watch their weight or lose weight, the problem can start simply by giving up all desserts, which is socially acceptable and not uncommon. Next a loved one is reading labels on all foods, counting calories, weighing himself or herself several times a day, exercising more and more, throwing food away or hiding it, making every excuse for not having an appetite, not eating, or participating in any number of possible eating disorder behaviors.

After my blame and guilt subsided enough for me to look deeper into the causation, I demanded an explanation and better insight into how a person could "allow" himself or herself to starve, and why. What about the physical pain of hunger? What about the lethargy and fogginess produced by low blood sugar? How could my girls have such willpower? Was it really perfectionism taking over? The type A personality gone awry? While these are prevalent themes in the discussions of eating disorders, what I discovered is none of the above are what led my daughters to starve. Now, what I understand about eating disorders, thanks to the leading researchers and authors in the field, has not only enabled me to get to the bottom of why my daughters developed this illness, it has become the antidote that keeps my daughters consciously aware of their illness and that sustains their recoveries.

Could This Be an Eating Disorder?

Significant eating disordered behaviors and life-threatening medical conditions may develop in a relatively short time: loss of menstruation, hair loss, physical weakness, dehydration, alarmingly low blood pressure, lowered body temperature, and many other serious medical problems. And this doesn't even consider the severe mood changes.

Some eating disorders develop gradually while others can become very serious, quite rapidly. Even if developed gradually, over a longer period of time, those eating disordered behaviors have still been practiced for a long time, and it will likely take longer to replace them with positive behaviors and to relearn normal eating.

Perhaps you can even prevent the onset of a full-blown eating disorder by catching it early, before it progresses any further. Don't take the "wait and see if this gets better" approach; chances are it won't, and the risks are far too high to take that chance. It's no different than any progressive disease or illness—early intervention is key. Cancer, a heart condition, or even a bunion is always better caught early since the disease or condition becomes more difficult to treat as it progresses. The condition may only worsen over time, while other potentially serious medical problems may develop on top of the eating disorder.

Right now, though, is not the time to dwell on possible causes or ignore your concerns, but instead to take immediate action. Assist and encourage your loved one to seek professional help. As the National Eating Disorders Association (NEDA) says, "Treatment is available. Recovery is possible."

STOP THE BLAME GAME

I was the first (and only) person I wanted to beat up on when I finally admitted my daughters had eating disorders. It is our natural propensity as parents to blame ourselves. But an eating disorder is no one's fault. Parents often feel they have caused the eating disorder. In fact, any caregiver may feel responsible. But here is the truth about eating disorders. According to experts, parents are not the cause. In fact, treatment programs are now providing evidenced-based treatment that is *family-based* or *family-centered*, taking the position that families are not the problem but instead an important part of the solution.

Individuals suffering from an eating disorder are not to blame either. They did not choose to develop an eating disorder. Eating disorders are not a choice nor are they intentional. As mentioned earlier, contrary to popular belief, they are not caused by vanity or an individual's willpower. They are biologically based-brain illnesses.

Signs and Symptoms

Based on my personal experiences and readings, the following are common indicators, personality traits, or signs of an eating disorder:

- Weight loss
- Self-starvation

COULD THIS BE AN EATING DISORDER?

- Eats only healthy foods
- Excessively counts calories or fat grams
- People pleasing
- Overachieving
- Frequently weighs self
- Obsessively reads cookbooks
- Increased interest in cooking or baking
- Limits portions significantly
- Restricts eating
- Perfectionism
- Expresses comments or concerns about body image
- Low self-esteem
- Overexercising
- Depression
- Fears gaining weight
- Hides or throws away food
- Expresses thoughts of suicide
- Demonstrates rigid, inflexible thinking
- Experiences difficulty making choices and frequently seeks others' opinions

- Frequently searches Internet, magazines, cookbooks, etc., for pictures of food
- Exhibits unusual behaviors (such as crumbling, mixing, or pushing food to certain places on the plate)
- Has routines or rituals around eating
- Frequently seeks reassurance
- Participates in other forms of self-harm, such as cutting, scratching, taking drugs or alcohol
- Denies being hungry
- Is dishonest about eating
- Searches Internet for information on losing weight
- Withdrawals socially
- Reduced concentration
- Declining performance at school or work
- Reports symptoms of dizziness or fainting
- Irritability
- Misusing laxatives
- Uses bathroom during or after meals frequently
- Sore throat
- Wears oversized clothing

Could This Be an Eating Disorder?

- Comments that he/she is overweight, when clearly not
- Comments about disliking certain parts of their body
- Uses appetite suppressants or diet pills
- Binge eats
- Self-induces vomiting after eating
- Appears stressed and overwhelmed
- Expresses disliking self
- Stashes food
- Large amounts of food are missing
- Feels cold; they report feeling cold frequently or you notice they need to wear warmer clothing than expected and use extra blankets
- Secretive eating
- Considerable fluctuations in weight
- Difficulty sleeping
- Reduced interest in activities previously enjoyed
- Expresses feeling hopeless
- Decreased interest in personal grooming

While this extensive list presents common symptoms, it does not exhaust all the possible symptoms of an eating disorder. Watching one's weight, dieting, exercising to avoid weight gain, counting calories, overindulging on occasion are common among individuals who do not have eating disorders. What differentiates someone with an eating disorder is the compulsive nature of eating behaviors. A person suffering from an eating disorder may exhibit any combination of symptoms. A symptom may also be exhibited by your loved one that is not listed above.

For instance, our younger daughter said she initially searched the Internet to "just look at pictures of foods, especially my favorites, to help me not feel hungry." Early in her illness, she did this to satisfy her hunger. Later, when she dropped considerable weight and was in what is referred to by leading experts as a state of negative energy balance (to be discussed further), she lost her hunger cues all together and no longer needed to engage in this activity.

I have yet to come across "searching the Internet to look at foods as a means of satisfying hunger" as a behavioral symptom of an eating disorder, but I added it to provide an example of a symptom *you* may notice in your loved one, but may not have previously read or learned about. If the behavior concerns you, consider that behavior an indication of a potential problem.

Additionally, someone may exhibit a symptom listed above and not have an eating disorder. Again, seek professional help to determine if indeed there's a problem and to obtain the necessary recommendations.

Medical Side Effects

Serious medical conditions can develop as a result of the eating disorder behaviors. From my personal experience with my daughters and from reading on the subject, the following are medical conditions or complications that may develop:

- Dehydration
- Loss of muscle and weakness
- Reduced bone density (osteopenia or osteoporosis)
- Dry skin
- Dizziness or fainting
- Development of lanugo (hair) all over the body to provide warmth
- Reduced heart rate
- Low blood pressure
- Loss of menstruation
- Anemia
- Infertility
- Sore throat
- Mouth sores

- Dental problems (caused by the increase in acid from self-induced vomiting)
- Hair thinning and loss
- Gastrointestinal problems (such as GI reflux, esophagitis, gastroparesis, and constipation)
- Kidney failure
- Electrolyte imbalance (may lead to heart problems, including heart arrhythmias and death)
- Heart failure
- Hypertension
- Heart disease
- Type 2 diabetes

These medical conditions are serious and potentially life threatening, further supporting the need to seek professional help as soon as possible. If symptoms are just emerging, then hopefully recovery will require less time and effort as well as increase the chance of a full recovery. If the problems are further along, getting professional help as soon as possible is essential to restore the individual's weight, normalize eating behaviors, treat underlying psychological issues or problems, and prevent the onset of serious and potentially life-threatening medical complications.

The first step toward awareness is acceptance and asking yourself, *Could this be an eating disorder?* It's the beginning of what can be a journey of discovery, empowerment, and understanding that will assist you in building a dream team of professionals, family, and friends that will help you assist your loved one in recovery.

You will read how there are no two eating disorders alike. They are by nature as individual and unique as the person they plague. For that reason, it is to be expected that where you are in your struggle with your loved one, whether you have intervened, sought professional help, or had the necessary hard talk, also varies greatly. Therefore, I have organized this book so that you can easily access information that you believe is applicable to your loved one's stage of recovery, whether you are still grappling with answering the question, *Could This Be an Eating Disorder?* or are already supporting your loved one in a specialized Family-Centered Treatment (FCT) facility, or providing Family-Based Treatment (FBT) at home.

Part I offers what I have learned through hands-on experience, interviews with specialists, and tons of my own research about understanding this enigmatic disease. What exactly is it, what classifies an illness as an eating disorder, what is the cause, and, most important, how to begin to understand or empathize with the eating disordered mind.

If your situation is grave, you can jump to part II, which takes readers through the challenges and strategies of talking with their loved one about getting help (without defensiveness, blame, judgment, or arguing), what kinds of treatments are available, how to determine which treatment is right for your loved one, as well as what to do and what not to do while you play an active role in your loved one's recovery process. Upon picking up the phone and placing that first call to get my girls help, I remember just how quickly my sense of doom transformed into a sense of confidence in my girls' ability to get well. This single step helped me evolve from feeling paralyzed by fear and concern to being encouraged and positive about the future. If this book is *your* single step, I want you to know there is hope; there is recovery. The process you are about to embark on is arduous but ultimately can be a transformative gift to your loved one and your entire family. This book and other available resources will assist you in learning what you need to know in order to participate in the recovery process in an effective, responsible way.

PART I

What We Now Know About Eating Disorders

WHAT'S INSIDE:

Important Concepts

Eating Disorder Basics

Why Is This Happening?

The Enigmatic Aspects of a Mysterious Disease

Getting Clear on Distorted Body Image

The Eating Disordered Mind and Change in Personality

CHAPTER 1

Important Concepts

In this chapter, concepts will be discussed that have been particularly enlightening for me, someone not directly experiencing the illness, but desperately trying to understand to help someone I love to recover and maintain her recovery. These concepts will be referred to often throughout this book, so they are presented here to help you in your understanding as you read on and process the information.

Similarities with Addictions

Here is an interesting aspect that was especially helpful for me. Eating disorders share similarities with addictions. Lauren Goldhamer holds an M.Ed. in Counseling Psychology and is an Eating Disorder Specialist and writes, "There are a number of ways in which different eating disorder behaviors fit the process definition of addiction. For example, people with eating disorders:

- Have difficulty controlling 'use' of food or behaviors
- Continue their behaviors despite evidence that it is harmful and may have serious emotional, social, and health-related consequences
- Put off or neglect important activities
- Experience a preoccupation with the 'substance,' which in this case is food

There are other similarities between addictions and eating disorders. For instance:

- Just as one drink can trigger an alcoholic into further drinking, a 'trigger' food can induce episodes of binge eating
- Sometimes people with anorexia say their self-starvation brings on an altered state they liken to being 'high'
- Bingeing and purging can bring on a feeling of 'release'
- Denial of the problem is a common feature of both substance use and eating disorders."

(Goldhamer, 2009)

It should be noted that the second similarity listed above may be compromised, at least initially while malnourished, for those struggling with anorexia nervosa due

Important Concepts

to a condition called anosognosia. Lauren Muhlheim, Clinical Psychologist and Certified Eating Disorder Specialist, writes, "Anosognosia, or lack of awareness, has an anatomical basis and is caused by damage to the brain." Muhlheim continues, "Applying the term anosognosia to anorexia nervosa makes sense because we know the brain is affected by malnutrition." Another important distinction is that "denial," the last similarity listed above, may actually not be denial in the case of anorexia nervosa. Muhlheim clarifies, "anosognosia is a brain condition; it is not the same as denial. Fortunately, the brain recovers with renourishment." (Muhlheim, 2016).

Another similarity noted in the literature, is that many individuals report experiencing their eating disorder like an addiction. Dr. Timothy Walsh, M.D., an Eating Disorder Researcher and Professor of Psychiatry at Columbia University Medical Center states, "Many people have noticed that when people with eating disorders—bulimia in general—talk about the foods they binge on, it can sound a lot like how people with substance abuse problems talk about abusing drugs" (Quittner, 2011).

According to the website eatingdisorderhope.com, research recently conducted shows commonalities between eating disorders and addictive conditions, such as drug addiction and alcoholism. In fact, the American Society of Addiction Medicine now considers addiction to include not only drugs and alcohol, but "process" addictions, such as food: "This is mostly due to the effect that all of these substances and behaviors have on the brain" (Ross, 2012).

We have reward centers in the brain, and a chemical reaction of pleasure can be produced from drugs of all kinds, alcohol, and eating disorders, such as bingeing, or employing behaviors to maintain a state of self-starvation. Starvation (a state of negative energy balance, to be discussed further) is said to send messages of pleasure, antianxiety, a sense of calm. In Dr. Walsh's recommendation, "I think it's very important to continue to pursue the neurobiology of addictions to substances and the neurobiology of eating disorders, and really try to understand how the neurobiological systems are affected . . . What's similar and what's different—that's the key. It would be very helpful in understanding and treatment if we understood those in more detail" (Quittner, 2011).

While many researchers and experts acknowledge the similarities that eating disorders have to addictions, they also note differences. Dr. Walsh explains, "Experts tend to avoid the term 'addiction' when talking about eating disorders because treatment is so different" (Quittner, 2011). Lauren Goldhamer concurs as she states, ". . . in treating eating disorders, individuals need help in challenging the issues specific to their eating disorder, and these are not entirely discussed by any addictions model." Goldhamer specifies that individuals "need help correcting negative thoughts and feelings regarding body image . . . they also need help and support while going through the process of changing their relationship with food" (Goldhamer, 2011). Furthermore, Dr. Walsh expands, "Although addicts try never to use or consume drugs or alcohol again,

Important Concepts

people with bulimia must learn how to have a more normal relationship with food, and to eat for nutrition" (Qittner, 2011).

Allow me to be perfectly clear, I am not claiming eating disorders are addictions. As mentioned above, experts are aware of similarities, but note clear differences and believe further research in this area is warranted.

I believe families should also be aware that eating disorders and substance abuse often co-occur. Amy Baker Dennis, Ph.D., and Bethany Helfman, Psy. D., expert contributors of the National Eating Disorders Association (NEDA)'s website, report that "Research suggests that nearly 50% of individuals with an eating disorder (ED) are also abusing drugs and/or alcohol, a rate 5 times greater than what is seen in the general population."

These experts point out another interesting similarity, "Substance abuse, like eating disorders, are influenced by genetic, biological, environmental, and psychological factors . . . Multiple shared neurotransmitters are thought to be involved in both eating and substance use disorders."

It is also not my intention to simplify eating disorders by noting certain aspects that resemble addictions. Research has made great strides in better understanding that eating disorders are not simple at all but are instead complex mental illnesses. According to the National Institute of Mental Health (NIMH), "eating disorders are caused by a complex interaction of genetic, biological, behavioral, psychological, and social factors."

My reasoning for discussing the similarities between

eating disorders and addictions is two-fold. Discussing the similarities is not for the assistance you offer your loved one. It is not intended for helping the person with the eating disorder. Instead, it is presented to help you better understand and appreciate the powerful nature of eating disorders. The pleasure, sense of calm, soothing feeling the individual craves from the eating disorder anorexia is one element of a complex mental illness, which has many contributing components. The behaviors associated with other eating disorders such as binge eating and bulimia are difficult for sufferers to resist and can feel overpowering. This understanding may help you in your attempts to be patient and empathetic; to think or suggest it is as easy as "just stop" or "just eat" becomes understandably unrealistic when considered through this perspective. Secondly, I feel it is imperative for family members to be aware of the high co-occurrence of eating disorders and substance abuse.

Negative Energy Balance

Dr. Cynthia Bulik, distinguished professor and researcher in the area of genetics of anorexia nervosa at the University of North Carolina at Chapel Hill, describes that self-starvation actually feels different to someone with anorexia; it "confers a sense of calm," "it is alluring to them . . . because it is anxiolytic" (reduces anxiety). When something helps us feel better, we tend to crave it, whatever it is; in the case of anorexia nervosa it occurs from a

IMPORTANT CONCEPTS

state of starvation. As mentioned in the previous section of this chapter, Goldhamer reports, "Sometimes people with anorexia say their self-starvation brings on an altered state they liken to being 'high.'"

For those intentionally wanting to slim down and lose weight, behaviors that seem to be relatively normal and harmless to start, such as giving up all desserts or counting calories, can quickly lead to weight loss, putting the individual into a state of negative energy balance. This negative energy balance may have a calming, pleasurable effect, making the behaviors of restricting, purging, or overexercising more frequent and self-perpetuating, therefore sparking an eating disorder in those predisposed to anorexia. According to Bulik, the state of starvation creates a negative energy balance, which is a "physical experience that is different in people prone to anorexia."

For those prone or predisposed to anorexia nervosa, hunger is calming and gives them a false, paradoxical "sense of well-being": a "positive biological reaction." This differs from the "misguided explanations [of anorexia nervosa] that focus on control, willpower, and even stubbornness," reports Bulik.

Julie O'Toole, M.D., Founder and Chief Medical Officer of Kartini Clinic, an internationally recognized pediatric eating disorder treatment program in Portland, Oregon, further explains that for "a person who does not have the brain chemistry associated with this eating disorder," hunger is unpleasant, food is calming, and food "improves mood."

Writes Bulik, "The starvation state is alluring to them, not because it signals weight loss, but because it is anxiolytic. That means that negative energy balance actually confers a sense of calm on their otherwise unsettled biology."

Predispositon

Although this concept is discussed in the preceding section and again in upcoming chapters, it's discussed here to help you assimilate this important concept. Having a genetic predisposition basically means you are susceptible or vulnerable to developing an eating disorder. This does not mean that if you are predisposed, you will develop an eating disorder. According to the National Institute of Mental Health (NIMH), "eating disorders are caused by a complex interaction of genetic, biological, behavioral, psychological, and social factors." The genetic component leads one to be predisposed or not.

Many people diet and lose weight; many people suffer significant weight loss from illness, from a medication side effect, from surgery; many people exercise to lose weight or prevent weight gain; yet most do not develop eating disorders. For the majority of us, being hungry or malnourished is unpleasant and we seek to satisfy our hunger and renourish ourselves. Remember for those predisposed to develop anorexia nervosa, the state of starvation leads to a different, opposite sensation; for them it is a positive physical experience.

Another example of this predisposition relates to binge

eating. Many people have overindulged on food at some time in their life; yet for the majority this does not develop into a recurrent behavior resulting in the illness of bulimia nervosa or a binge eating disorder.

Unintentional Weight Loss and Anorexia

Lauren Muhlheim writes, "Some of the biggest misunderstandings about Anorexia Nervosa center around it being an intentional illness and related to vanity." In her research review of individuals being prone or vulnerable to anorexia, they "may need only weight loss from any source to result in clinical AN" (anorexia nervosa). Dr. Muhlheim in her article, *"Unintentional" Onset of Anorexia,* quotes researchers, "It was only after the unintended weight loss had occurred that the patient developed the desire to lose more weight or maintain the unsought lower weight."

"It is now believed that people with a genetic vulnerability to anorexia respond aberrantly to negative energy balance, allowing anorexia to develop," states Muhlheim.

This article mentions numerous causes for weight loss beyond intentionally dieting to lose weight; unintentional weight-loss reasons include healthy eating, overtraining for athletics, dietary changes such as becoming a vegetarian or vegan, and illness.

Muhlheim profoundly writes, "Since anorexia nervosa is an illness and not a choice, perhaps a more apt title would have been 'Unintentional Weight Loss as a Trigger for Anorexia.'"

This was exactly what occurred with Jillian and something I wish more people understood. We never heard comments from Jillian about wanting to lose weight, slim down, or diet. Jillian's initial weight loss was unintentionally brought on by heightened anxiety and stress. It was Amelia's illness (mono) that caused her initial unintended weight loss that then triggered her anorexia and her desire to lose more weight. I was under the mistaken impression that those desires for weight loss, to be skinny . . . were a necessary component of anorexia. This lack of knowledge played a role in our delay in recognizing the problem and seeking help. Parents and families should recognize that weight loss may occur *unintentionally,* but that weight loss can actually spark the development of anorexia nervosa.

CHAPTER 2

Eating Disorder Basics

No two eating disorders are alike. Each one is as individual as the person it plagues. While there are commonalities, eating disorders and recoveries vary and are highly personalized. Obviously as human beings we bring with us to every situation our own lens on things. Our personalities are different and the relationships with family and friends are also personal. They say that no two children are alike, and I can attest to that. Like most siblings, our daughters are wonderfully unique. They differ in so many ways; even their eating disorders were drastically different.

Jillian

Our oldest daughter, Jillian, had perfectionist qualities and low self-esteem, and lacked confidence. She was also a people pleaser, overachiever, apprehensive, and anxious. As an entering high school freshman, her anxiety and obsessive-compulsive tendencies escalated. She developed rigid, inflexible thinking and ritualistic behaviors. Initially, we sought individual psychotherapy for her anxiety, which utilized Cognitive Behavioral Therapy (CBT), specifically exposure therapy. Jillian's obsessive-compulsive tendencies intensified and crept further into her eating habits. She has a serious food allergy to tree nuts and has been a vegetarian since age seven, while the rest of us eat a variety of foods. Her obsession grew to a point where I was not allowed to plate her food or pack her lunch; she was constantly in the kitchen while I cooked, criticized my hand hygiene, and obsessed whether everything was nut free, meat free, and void of meat by-products.

What she learned as a child about good hygiene and nutrition, Jillian took to intense levels. If other family members suggested avoiding processed foods and eating whole, all-natural foods, she was an all-or-nothing student. I wouldn't say that our daughter's food allergy *caused* her eating disorder. As I have learned, eating disorders are far more complex than that, and plenty of individuals have serious food allergies and do not develop eating disorders. However, it is possible that our teaching Jillian to stay clear of tree nuts due to the seriousness of her food allergy prompted her rigidity and anxiety. We were often worried that she may have another anaphylactic reaction, especially when she was away from the safety of home.

Jillian's thinking about food and eating became increasingly inflexible. It appears that as her anxiety and stress increased, she began to lose weight, and a downward spiral ensued. I witnessed Jillian becoming more and more rigid and ritualistic around food. The more she starved her brain of vital nutrients, the more she participated in behaviors that further led her to restrict. She was caught in a vicious cycle of negative energy balance, a concept detailed in the previous chapter. Her brain chemistry and functioning became altered due to malnutrition, and she just continued to deteriorate. For Jillian, this state of starvation inappropriately stimulated her brain's reward centers, literally making it stop functioning the way it was supposed to. So, instead of an unpleasant response (like feeling hungry or irritable), my usually anxious daughter experienced a sense of calm and well-being when she was restricting and starving herself (Bulik, C., Ph.D.). Although Jillian was striving for a sense of control, her illness was actually in control of her and her eating.

Facing her eating disorder was a challenging time for Jillian (likely the biggest challenge she will ever face), but I am blessed to report that she has recovered from her eating disorder *and* OCD. She is attending college out of state— something we never imagined possible for her just five and a half years ago. Now, she is an exceedingly confident and capable young woman, unrecognizable from the meek and troubled high school freshman she once was. Knowledge is power, and Jillian now understands that the effect weight loss has on her is very different from how it reacts in the chemistry and brain functioning of those not predisposed to anorexia. Therefore, she must be diligent in this regard to sustain her recovery. Essentially, she must prevent any weight loss (intentional or unintentional) that could lead to a negative energy balance and send her into a relapse. She understands and accepts that anorexia is a biological brain disorder, and that she is predisposed to this illness.

Amelia

At the time Jillian was restricting, losing weight, and becoming ill with an eating disorder, her sister, two years younger and barely a teenager, was recovering from the viral illness mononucleosis. Amelia missed a lot of school, and all the downtime led to depression. She overheard lots of heated conversations (to put it mildly) between her older sister and me, as we tried to understand why Jillian was not eating and was losing weight. Amelia began to focus her attention on considering her own weight and size. She had memories of being teased and told hurtful things about her body, such as being chubby as a young girl, which she kept private and let fester within. Amelia, for many years, struggled silently with body image issues. The mono resulted in her initial weight loss, which made it easier for Amelia to blame the drastic change in her body on the virus. I took her to see many doctors to determine why she wasn't getting better, why she was losing weight and only getting weaker instead of better. While it was true that initially the virus caused her weakness and some weight loss, later she was secretly restricting and overexercising while she was home alone and sick (with what we believed was an extended illness from mono). It is likely that her eating disorder was triggered by an unintentional weight loss as an onset or trigger for anorexia (Muhlheim, L., Psy.D.). Amelia's unintended weight loss led to a negative energy balance, and the calming sensation she experienced led her to starve more. Based on Amelia's personal reports and my experience with her during this time, it appears the changes in her brain as a result of this state of starvation led to her thoughts becoming more obsessive about wanting to restrict, lose weight, and not get fat. Her thoughts became increasingly distorted, especially regarding her body image. Peers' and adults' comments like, "You look so good, you look so skinny," only fueled her motivation. Because Amelia resisted gaining weight, she became fearful and anxious toward food and eating.

Amelia's road to recovery differed greatly from her older sister's recovery. Body image issues, body checking, and comparing herself to her sister have significantly improved but remain a challenge. In recovery, Amelia has developed coping strategies and skills, improved communication skills, and self-awareness. In many ways, she is mature beyond her years and demonstrates incredibly keen perception and insight into herself, her relationships, and her experiences. These are some unexpected positive outcomes from her efforts in recovery, and I am confident they will serve her well her entire life.

The Five Categories of Eating Disorders

As experts learn more, classifications change and new disorders are identified. According to the American

Psychiatric Association's (APA) most recent publication of the Diagnostic and Statistical Manual of Mental Disorders (DSM-5), the following are the five categories of eating disorders:

1. Anorexia Nervosa

Anorexia is self-starvation (*an*, meaning without, and *orexia*, meaning appetite). Much continues to be learned about the causation of anorexia. Scientific research in genetics and neurobiology is supporting that there are biological reasons for the development of anorexia nervosa. Dr. Thomas Insel, from the National Institute of Mental Health (NIMH), states, anorexia is a "brain disorder" with a "genetic factor" (Insel, 2009). This genetic factor doesn't cause anorexia, but it puts someone at risk for developing the illness. Dr. Cynthia Bulik, distinguished professor and researcher in the area of genetics of anorexia nervosa at the University of North Carolina at Chapel Hill, describes that the state of starvation creates a negative energy balance, which is a "physical experience that is different in people prone to anorexia." This is the negative energy balance I mentioned that presented in both of my daughters. Interestingly, anorexia nervosa may be triggered by an intentional weight loss (such as dieting), but oftentimes it develops from an unintentional weight loss (such as from an illness, medication side effects, surgery).

For those prone to anorexia nervosa, hunger is calming and gives them a false, paradoxical "sense of well-being"; a "positive biological reaction." This differs from the

EATING DISORDER BASICS

"misguided explanations [of anorexia nervosa] that focus on control, willpower, and even stubbornness," reports Bulik.

Julie O'Toole, M.D., Founder and Chief Medical Officer of Kartini Clinic, an internationally recognized pediatric eating disorder treatment program in Portland, Oregon, further explains that for "a person who does not have the brain chemistry associated with this eating disorder," hunger is unpleasant, food is calming, and food "improves mood."

Writes Bulik, "The starvation state is alluring to them, not because it signals weight loss, but because it is anxiolytic. That means that negative energy balance actually confers a sense of calm on their otherwise unsettled biology. What makes the rest of us more anxious makes them less. Obviously, the job of providers is to help them be able to achieve that sense of calm in other ways—ways that are not physically harmful." As someone supporting recovery, some important points to keep in mind are:

1. Your loved one is not being difficult, stubborn, or demonstrating willpower. Someone cannot choose to be anorexic. It's a brain disease. People are not to blame and they should not be made to feel guilty.

2. Anorexia nervosa is a brain-based illness and is triggered when a predisposed individual experiences a negative energy balance in the brain, either intentionally (such as from dieting) or unintentionally (such as from an illness, surgery, medications, or stress).

3. Due to the false calming and antianxiety sensations produced in the brain during a state of negative energy balance, a person may seek that "pleasure," and perpetuate behaviors that extend it.

4. It is critically important that your loved one avoid negative energy balances during and after recovery. To do this, you can assist and educate your loved one to be resolute in the prevention of weight loss to support recovery, sustain recovery, and prevent relapse.

5. Someone with anorexia may practice unhealthy behaviors such as restricting calories, only eating specific foods, or skipping meals frequently; purging; and/or overexercising.

6. Due to the state of starvation, brain changes occur, which may alter a person's perception of reality. Often these individuals do not believe others when they are told they are too thin or too skinny because their self-perception no longer corresponds to reality. The individual may develop obsessive thoughts around needing to restrict or purge to avoid weight gain or to lose more weight. Often these individuals develop distorted body image—the image they see in the mirror is an altered image. This may be one of the most difficult aspects for loved ones to grasp and will be discussed further in Chapter 5: Getting Clear on Distorted Body Image. This may

Eating Disorder Basics

occur in addition to the antianxiety or positive sensations from the negative energy balance, making the illness only more powerful.

7. For some struggling with anorexia, if left to their own devices, they may not seek professional treatment nor actively participate in treatment and could become emaciated and even develop life-threatening medical conditions. Anosognosia (lack of insight or self-awareness) is commonly associated and likely due to the changes in brain functioning. This condition only further supports the need for treatment.

A diagnosis of anorexia nervosa is made by a physician when there is significant low body weight without a medical reason/explanation—the important attribute being the individual's inability to sustain a normal body weight. Any, or all of the following behaviors may be demonstrated by the individual: restricting, overexercising, and/or purging.

2. Bulimia Nervosa

Also a serious, potentially life-threatening eating disorder, bulimia is often less easily recognized since individuals suffering from it may or may not be underweight. From Greek *boulimia,* "ravenous hunger," bulimia is also called binge-purge syndrome because a person will consume large quantities of food in a short time, and then mitigate his or her feelings of shame by purging the food from the body. This disorder may be prompted by a desire to prevent weight gain and feeling ashamed for what he or she has eaten, as well as other emotions such as low self-esteem or a sense of worthlessness. Purging methods include self-induced vomiting and/or misusing laxatives or diuretics. Nonpurging activities include excessive exercising or fasting to undo a binge.

This disorder is difficult to notice because the purging is most often done privately or secretively. Loved ones should pay close attention to frequency of bathroom use during or after meals. This includes showers taken after meals, as some individuals purge in the shower for increased secretiveness. The chance for recovery increases with early detection. Therefore, it is important to be aware of some of the above-mentioned warning signs of bulimia nervosa and support your loved one in seeking professional help as soon as possible.

There are addiction similarities with the binge-eating portion of bulimia nervosa. Ashley Gearhardt, M.S., and colleagues wrote a paper, *Binge Eating and Food Addiction*. These experts note that the similarities between binge eating and addiction are the "diminished control and continued excessive consumption despite negative consequences." As presented earlier, Timothy Walsh, M.D., states, "many people have noticed that when people with eating disorders—bulimia in general—talk about the foods they binge on, it can sound a lot like how people with substance abuse problems talk about abusing drugs" (Quittner, 2011). If the individual struggling with bulimia (binging and purging) is underweight, then conceivably they, too, may experience the positive biological responses (calming, anti-anxiety effect) from negative energy balance, which may help explain their behaviors of purging, restricting, over-exercising, or overuse of laxatives.

3. Binge-Eating Disorder

Also referred to as compulsive overeating, an individual consumes large amounts of food, ignores fullness cues, and often reports the inability to stop eating when bingeing. This differs from bulimia in that the individual does not participate in purging to compensate for caloric intake; the individual also does not exercise excessively or fast after binging. The individual also suffers from having negative feelings for having participated in bingeing, such as shame, guilt, worthlessness, and/or feelings of depression. The individual may fluctuate between periods of binging and dieting and may or may not be overweight. Others may become overweight or obese with the associated health concerns and risks of obesity. The key attribute of a binge-eating disorder is the compulsive nature of the overeating (the inability to control the behavior). The addiction-like similarities, as with bulimia, being "the diminished control and continued excessive consumption despite negative consequences" (Gearhardt, 2011).

4. Other Specified Feeding or Eating Disorders (OSFED)

Previously known as Eating Disorders Not Otherwise Specified (EDNOS), Other Specified Feeding or Eating

Disorders (OSFED) are those that do not meet the criteria of anorexia, bulimia, or binge-eating disorder. These eating disorders may have serious detrimental effects both psychologically and physically. The individual may experience overwhelming concerns about his or her weight or size. While the individual does not meet exact criteria for a diagnosis of anorexia, bulimia, or binge-eating disorder, the eating disorder is serious, the individual may suffer to similar extents and require professional help. The types of eating disorders that fall in this category are:

- Atypical anorexia: presents with all of the same characteristics with the exception of the extent of weight-loss criteria.

- Bulimia presents with the same characteristics, but at a reduced frequency of occurrence.

- Binge-eating disorder presents with the same characteristics, but at a reduced frequency of occurrence.

- Purging disorder involves purging activities of self-induced vomiting or misuse of laxatives and diuretics, but without binge eating.

- Night-eating syndrome is eating excessive amounts of food at nighttime. According to DSM-5, this syndrome is defined as "recurrent episodes of night eating; eating after awakening from sleep; or by excessive food consumption after the evening meal."

5. Avoidant/Restrictive Food Intake Disorders (ARFID)

It is not necessarily a new problem, but it is newly recognized as an eating disorder in the DSM-5, which was published in May 2013. Sufferers of ARFID are defined as anyone with clinically significant struggles with food and eating. For children, these struggles are behaviors such as unhealthy restrictions in what they will eat, avoiding certain colors or textures to the extent that they are not eating enough. Some children develop this from fear after a frightening experience like choking or food poisoning. Symptoms of ARFID can continue into adulthood and may result in significant weight loss and lead to the numerous problems related to not maintaining a healthy weight.

STATISTICS

The following are important and alarming statistics about eating disorders and recovery:

- It's estimated that 30 million individuals in the United States suffer from eating disorders, according to the National Association of Anorexia Nervosa and Associated Disorders (ANAD).

- As many as 13 percent of females struggle with eating disorders of anorexia, bulimia, and binge-eating disorders, according to the National Institute of Mental Health.

  This does not include those suffering with Other Specified Feeding and Eating Disorders.

- Ninety-five percent of individuals suffering eating disorders are between the ages of twelve and twenty-five, according to the Substance Abuse and Mental Health Services Administration, Offices of the U.S. Department of Health and Human Services.
- Renfrew Center Eating Disorders Treatment Facility reports that 20 percent of people suffering from anorexia will prematurely die from complications related to their eating disorder, including suicide and heart problems.
- Anorexia has the highest fatality rate of any mental illness (Arcelus, 2011).

I certainly appreciate what a devastating time this may be for you and your loved one. An eating disorder can wreak havoc on an entire family. Those days and months surrounding the height of my daughters' illnesses were the darkest, most hopeless, and most challenging time in my life. I did not believe life would ever be the same again.

While the research studies report the efficacy of treatment and skilled professionals are reassuring, take it from me, recovery *is* possible. Your loved one can be successful in overcoming this illness and live a normal, happy, fulfilling life. However, he or she will need your positive attitude and your unwavering commitment to recovery.

CHAPTER 3

Why Is This Happening?

It is common to feel responsible for having caused your loved one's eating disorder, but as mentioned earlier, while there could be many answers to the desperate question "why is this happening," one thing is certain: research supports the fact that families *do not* cause eating disorders. Unfortunately when we were most vulnerable and distraught, my husband was the brunt of accusations from some family members blaming him for having "caused the girls' eating disorders." While I considered him the most fun-loving and devoted father, and anything but the cause of their problems, Joe had to carry this burden around during an exceedingly difficult time. To an already devastated and distraught father, the lack of support and insurmountable judgment was an incredible emotional blow. I knew he wasn't responsible, and I did my very best to assure him of that.

Instead of trying to educate such unhelpful family members, I focused my attention on taking care of my immediate family. Doing otherwise would have been a negative distraction and unworthy of my valuable time and energy. Besides, parents often do enough self-blaming on their own and certainly do not need it from other family members. In fact, it's the exact opposite of what parents need when their child is facing an eating disorder.

Although I knew without a doubt that my husband was not to blame, I did my share of self-blaming. Imagine how I felt! It had to be me—their mother, the one who nursed them as babies, taught them to feed themselves, and their "cook"—who caused this. I have two children, and *both* develop eating disorders? This tormented me. What was it that I was doing wrong? Prior to our daughters joining one of our weekly family sessions with our treatment team, I sheepishly raised my concerns. All of the professionals reassured me that I did not cause my daughters' eating disorders. The psychiatrist gave me an insightful explanation. She indicated that many moms are constantly dieting, emphatic about exercising, pore over nutrition labels, complain about their weight, size, and the way clothes fit; in spite of it all, they don't have children who develop eating disorders. I knew I was not a mom who was constantly concerned about my weight or size. I did not overexercise, nor did I only feed my family healthy food. We had our share of desserts and treats. I was not a bad example or role model in this regard. We were, and remain to be, a close family and enjoy spending time together. There were no unusual family issues, stressors, or trauma I was aware of that could have caused the disorder.

In 2009, the Academy of Eating Disorders (AED)

released a position paper stating that there is no data to support anorexia or bulimia being caused by a certain type of parenting, saying, "AED stands firmly against any etiologic model of eating disorders in which family influences are seen as the primary cause of anorexia nervosa or bulimia nervosa and condemns generalizing statements that imply families are to blame for their child's illness." The experts and authors of this paper further state, "theories of causation are now recognized as overly simplistic and erroneous" (Le Grange, D., Lock, J., and colleagues, 2009). Furthermore, it is the position of the AED that there is "increasing evidence that heritable influences underlie susceptibility to both anorexia nervosa and bulimia nervosa."

Okay, so if I wasn't the cause of their eating disorders and there were no family issues that I was aware of, then what was the cause?

What We Currently Know About Causation

According to the National Institute of Mental Health (NIMH), "eating disorders are caused by a complex interaction of genetic, biological, behavioral, psychological, and social factors." Experts in the field of eating disorders have determined that the illness lives in the brain and certain individuals are prone to eating disorders due to genetics; genetics are a risk factor. The triggering component for anorexia is negative energy balance ("mismatch between energy expended and energy taken in") that has a very different effect in an individual predisposed to anorexia nervosa. As presented previously, negative energy balance (self-starvation from behaviors such as restricting or purging) has an anxiolytic (antianxiety), soothing, or calming effect (Bulik, 2014). Jessica Baker describes that for most people, "appetite is simple, one gets hungry and then one eats. In the brain, appetite is a very complicated system of excitatory and inhibitory chemical reactions that involve hormones, senses, and a constant analysis of the levels of different nutrients in the bloodstream. When a person has an eating disorder, elements of this appetite system can be compromised or not functioning as they did before. Anxiety may take the place of hunger, or feeling full may take the place of feeling empty. Eating less can begin to feel soothing and pleasant" (Baker, 2015). This knowledge is important for you, as someone supporting recovery, because it can assist you in supporting your loved one in a few ways. Understanding negative energy balance and its role in eating disorders can help prevent blaming and guilt (on the part of yourself and your loved one battling the eating disorder). Second, and in my opinion more important, you can assist your loved one in being "vigilant," as Cynthia Bulik describes it, in avoiding a negative energy balance (intentional or unintentional weight loss) to sustain recovery and prevent relapse.

Eating disorders are complex illnesses. Jessica Baker, Ph.D., Associate Research Director for the Center of Excellence for Eating Disorders in the Department of Psychiatry at the University of North Carolina at Chapel Hill, reports that while there is a "genetic component, that is not to say that there is not an environmental effect . . . genetic factors likely work in combination with environmental effects to increase risk." Baker goes on to explain, "Many individuals in the world are exposed to the cultural thin ideal, but comparatively few people ever develop an eating disorder. Genetic factors may help us identify why some individuals are more vulnerable to environmental triggers."

The example is given that many people go on weight-loss diets, but only those with a greater predisposition go on to develop anorexia. Baker offers an insightful example supporting predisposition in the development of eating disorders, saying, "Similarly, just about everyone overeats at some point in their life, but those with higher genetic risk may be the ones for whom overeating can trigger recurrent binge eating episodes."

SUIT UP YOUR ARMOR

It's important to be mindful and self-aware, but do not blame yourself or anyone else. In fact, I recommend protecting yourself from anyone in your life who is judgmental or ignorantly participates in blaming versus being supportive of both you and the person struggling with the eating disorder. Instead, seek people who can offer the support you need, consider attending a support group, or even therapy for yourself. Remember this is a challenging time for you as well. Practice self-care. The more supported you feel and the better you take care of yourself, the more capable you will be in supporting your

> loved one during recovery. Modeling healthy behaviors and accepting help are excellent examples for the person in recovery.

There are several known contributing factors that may lead to the development of an eating disorder. Based on both personal experience and readings, the following are contributing factors or risk factors.

Genetic/Biological Risk Factors

- Genetic risk factors: research is revealing that eating disorders may be inherited; individuals may be predisposed for developing an eating disorder (Striegel-Moore, 2007).
- A coexisting problem in the individual such as depression, anxiety, or addiction.
- A medical condition that requires close attention or restriction of foods (such as food allergies, celiac disease, or diabetes).
- Family history of depression, anxiety, or addiction.

Psychological/Personality Characteristics

Just as individuals with eating disorders are all unique, their eating disorders are unique. The following are common characteristics of individuals with eating disorders:

Why Is This Happening?

- People pleaser
- Perfectionism
- Seeks reassurance
- Low self-esteem
- Low self-confidence
- Overachiever
- Nervous/anxious
- Inflexible or rigid thinking (i.e., "it can only be this way" type of thinking)

Coexisting Problems Risk Factors

- Anxiety
- Depression
- Obsessive-compulsive disorder
- Reduced coping skills

Environmental and Cultural Risk Factors

Before we discuss possible environmental and cultural risk factors, it is important to mention that it's a myth to consider eating disorders as only affecting affluent, young, Caucasian females. Eating disorders do not discriminate and affect people of all races, ages, socio-economic backgrounds, and genders. The following are potential risk factors pertaining to one's environment and culture.

- Family stress or trauma
- Life change (for example entering college or divorce)

- Activity or profession that requires or encourages certain physical appearance, weight, size (wrestling, gymnastics, ballet, or a career such as modeling or acting)

- Family dynamics (such as having high expectations, controlling or poor communication, emphasis on appearance, weight, or size)

- Another family member with an eating disorder

Our culture, as well as many other cultures around the world, places value on thinness. Individuals are pressured to look a certain way, receiving messages that say, in order to be considered beautiful or attractive, one needs to be thin. These standards of thinness displayed in the media are unrealistic, and usually the actors or models are not standard size. They are usually taller than average and below average weight for their height. If one compares himself or herself with those portrayed in magazines or catalogues, in movies or on TV, an individual may derive a false, negative self-image. The average woman in the United States is five-foot four inches and weighs 165 pounds; the average model is five-foot ten inches and weighs 107 pounds, according to the United States Centers for Disease Control and Prevention and Thoughtfulwoman.org.

It is important to note here that desired thinness as portrayed in the media and valued in society is a risk factor for those genetically predisposed to eating disorders. Individuals may desire a certain weight or size and participate in dieting activities. Remember many individuals go on weight-loss diets and do not develop eating disorders. A weight-loss diet, however, may lead to an eating disorder in those predisposed genetically. The diet may lead to a weight loss or a negative energy balance, again, triggering a very different biological response to the state of starvation than in those not predisposed. When expending more energy than consumed, these individuals do not become hungry, anxious, and/or irritable; instead they may experience a positive, antianxiety, calming response.

Interpersonal Risk Factors

- Reduced communication skills (for verbalizing feelings or showing emotions)

- Problems or strains in a relationship(s) with family or friend(s)

- Experiences with being teased or receiving unflattering comments about one's shape, size, or weight.

- Experience with trauma such as abuse, neglect, or death.

A Family Affair

While a family or friend can't cause an eating disorder, there may be factor(s) within a relationship that perpetuate the disorder. In treatment, it may be discovered that certain aspects of a particular relationship may need to be examined and possibly modified in an effort to support recovery. This relationship review is very different than the blame game. It is recognizing that the individual may need support or modifications within relationships. Treatment may uncover facets of a relationship that may require attention to support recovery. I recommend being open to explore your relationship with your loved one and your family dynamics; be mindful and self-aware. Again, this is different than blaming yourself or anyone else, and let me reiterate, research supports that families do not cause eating disorders. However, let me offer an example of how we needed to be open to our family dynamics and modify the way in which we interacted with our daughter to support her recovery.

Jillian, lacking confidence and being a people pleaser, was unable to make decisions, even the smallest ones, such as selecting what shoes to wear, how to style her hair, or whether she should do her homework before or after taking a shower. We routinely assisted her in making such decisions. Unknowingly, my husband and I perpetuated her inability to make decisions and develop independence and self-confidence. We were well meaning but unaware of this family dynamic. In fact, we enabled her lack of ability to make decisions. We didn't know that Jillian's frequent questions stemmed from her need for reassurance and low self-confidence, or that our catering to these needs were only doing her a disservice. Through introspection and therapy, we developed an awareness of our daughter's behaviors and our reactions. We determined that we needed to make adjustments in our interactions to facilitate her development.

Our acquired insight on how we operated interpersonally and as a family is an example of the importance of seeking professional help. Being so close to Jillian, we were unaware of these issues. The above example was not directly brought to my attention, but as I learned more about what Jillian was addressing in treatment, I recognized we could support her development in this area at home while she recovered. I encourage you to turn to the treatment team and be open—not defensive—in regard to relationship dynamics and how you can engage in recovery.

CHAPTER 4

The Enigmatic Aspects of a Mysterious Disease

Food is medicine. For individuals suffering from weight loss due to anorexia nervosa or bulimia nervosa, this fact is literally the case. In Family-Based Treatment (FBT) and the Family-Centered Treatment used in the different facilities where our daughters received care, weight restoration is the first focus of treatment. Food is the medicine that begins healing the brain and the body. We will discuss various treatment options further in Chapter 8.

According to Dr. Leslie Sim, psychologist specializing in eating disorders at Mayo Clinic's campus in Rochester, Minnesota, there isn't any "good pharmacology for anorexia; food is the medicine." With weight restoration, the individual's medical condition is stabilized with proper nutrition, and the individual's brain functioning improves; both are essential for the next phases of treatment and recovery.

It's likely an individual will not get better on his or her own. While it's not impossible to recover from an eating disorder without treatment, the greatest chance for recovery occurs with professional treatment. Experts stress the importance of early and aggressive treatment to improve the chances of a full recovery. As I learned, it wasn't *just a phase* and ignoring my concerns only made matters worse. My biggest regret is that I didn't address my concerns sooner. Ignoring my concerns certainly did not make them go away, but led to further deterioration while putting my daughters' lives at risk. In the case of other illnesses, such as cancer, we wouldn't wait for symptoms to progress or wait to see if the person gets better on his or her own, and we shouldn't wait for illnesses like anorexia nervosa either. Eating disorders are illnesses and require prompt intervention and your unwavering commitment to recovery.

The problem is that we can wrap our heads around illnesses like cancer and diabetes, even heart disease, but eating disorders are mysterious and difficult to conceptualize and rationalize. We want to understand the logic of starvation, but for many who aren't prone to eating disorders, no matter how hard we try to empathize, we can't imagine not eating. I needed to learn more about the aspects of eating disorders in order to engage more closely and accurately in my daughters' recoveries. There is still so much to learn and understand, especially because symptoms are so individualized; however, what I can tell you about this mysterious disease is that for sufferers, nothing makes more sense than the feeling of physical emptiness.

The Enigmatic Aspects of a Mysterious Disease

Distorted Body Image

The issue of distorted body image will only be touched on briefly as there is an entire chapter devoted to this aspect later in this book. The main point to be made here is that the distorted perception that a sufferer has of his or her body image is *real,* despite the reality that everyone else recognizes. This type of distorted perception cannot be compared to the wife that asks her husband, "Does this outfit make me look fat?" For many with distorted body image, what they see when they look at themselves in the mirror and what is actually the case can be completely different. Chapter 5: Getting Clear on Distorted Body Image will go into further detail and give you more insight into distorted body image. Hopefully, this information will prevent any further frustrations or heated conversations with you and your loved one. What your loved one sees and feels in regard to her size and shape is legitimate and real in her mind's eye.

Hunger Cues/Intuitive Eating

In simple terms, many individuals with eating disorders, primarily anorexia, lose their hunger cues. As hard as it is to believe, they simply do not feel hungry. This usually develops after significant weight loss has occurred. Therefore, when the individual tells you he or she is not hungry, trust your loved one is being honest and it is *real.* The individual does not feel hungry. The treatment team and family need to respond with understanding that the individual's assertions are legitimate. Your loved one is not just being difficult and stubborn. Your response should express both the understanding that he or she does not feel hungry and explanations on the reasons why he or she must eat regardless. Help your loved one understand that those normal inner body messages or cues are not working properly at this time. Inform your loved one that those normal, healthful messages have shut down temporarily because of the changes in his or her body. According to experts, "In the brain, appetite is a very complicated system of excitatory and inhibitory chemical reactions that involve different hormones, senses, and a constant analysis of the levels of different nutrients in the bloodstream. When people have an eating disorder, elements of this appetite system can be compromised or not functioning as they did before. Anxiety may take the place of hunger, or feeling full may take the place of feeling empty" (Baker, 2015). When you feel the time is appropriate, educate your loved one that those hunger cues and intuitive eating will return eventually once his or her health improves. But most important at this time, the emphasis should be placed on the necessity of eating regardless of feeling hungry; food is his or her medicine.

It took almost three-and-a-half years before those hunger cues returned for our older daughter. Hearing her expressing that she was "hungry" was a defining moment in her recovery. I remember that moment well. It had been so long since I heard her say those words. She said it so naturally as if she had never stopped saying it; it gave me pause and I had to ask myself, *did she just say she was hungry?* I celebrated silently and offered prayers of gratitude, then rattled off food suggestions from things we had available. I did my best to respond as naturally as I could to this perfectly ordinary comment.

The person suffering from an eating disorder can learn to eat and practice healthy behaviors related to eating without relying on hunger cues. The time it takes for hunger cues to return is not what's important; intuitive eating will return. Your takeaway here should be the awareness that your loved one may report not feeling hungry and that it is real. You will then be able to respond with empathy and provide sound and proven information as to why he or she needs to eat regardless of not feeling hungry.

Stand Strong Against the Eating Disorder

What is meant by suggesting that you stand strong against the eating disorder? First of all, it means to stand up to the illness, not to your loved one. This further supports the suggestion to separate the illness (the eating disorder) from the individual. From my experience, an eating disorder leads an individual to say and do things that they normally wouldn't. This is further discussed in Chapter 6: The Eating Disordered Mind and Change in Personality.

In support of recovery, you should go up against the eating disorder while remaining loving and compassionate toward your loved one. An example of this would be not backing down or giving into your loved one when he or she says something like, "I hate you! I'm not eating that. You are making me eat too much. You want me to get fat," and not backing down to his or her pleas to eat less, to eat something different, or his or her promises to eat more later. As hard as it may be, don't give in to your loved one even when he or she is throwing a fit or tantrum. Do your best to remain calm, loving, and compassionate, while standing strong. Try a response such as, "I know you feel full. That's expected. It will get better. Now, take another bite, you are almost done," or while handing the next spoonful to your loved one say something like, "I know this is hard. I see you are upset." Sure, he or she may only get angrier when his or her attempts fail, but in time these attempts cease; your loved one becomes less upset and complies with the expectations. It's as though the eating disorder (the illness) begins to lose control, and retreats.

TAMING THE BEAST

When our daughters were in partial hospitalization, eating two meals, five days a week in treatment, we were encouraged to eat with them during the evening meal. I was shocked to witness my daughters and the rest of the group adhering to the expectations without any resistance. They were expected to eat and drink everything at the meal. They were expected to bring their tray to the supervising therapist to verify they had finished. The girls stood there holding their tray while the therapist lifted, shook, and checked to ensure everything was consumed. At first I thought, *how humiliating!* but those in the group readily accepted these conditions.

I learned later that such supervision and expectations are indeed necessary to extinguish the eating disorder behaviors. The lesson here for us, as the support system, is to establish expectations and be consistent. This approach can be achieved calmly, with love and compassion, and should never be punitive. But to be effective, the expectations need to be expressed clearly and upheld.

More direct cues, such as "now drink your milk" or "you need to finish" stated tolerantly and patiently, work better than open-ended questions or choices, such as "what would you like to drink?" Early in recovering when focusing on weight restoration, I found avoiding questions around intake altogether worked best. Throughout treatment, we all learned to separate the eating disorder from the person it afflicts. And in doing so, we were able to disassociate the motivations and even the personality of the eating disorder from the motivations and personalities of our daughters. Some people find it helpful in personifying their eating disorder, as Jenni Schaefer so famously did by naming and referring to her eating disorder as "Ed." In her book, *Life Without Ed: How One Woman Declared Independence from Her Eating Disorder and How You Can Too*, Schaefer says this separation helped her treatment and recovery in many ways, one major one being it allowed her to defend herself from the negative thoughts and behaviors her addiction placed in her mind. She learned to understand the desire to starve was really "Ed" meddling in her recovery, like the little devil that shows up in the bubbles of our minds to argue with the angelic side of our brains. Ed, with his pitchfork, is there to fuel the addiction, to preserve his power over a person as he or she becomes mentally stronger, to sabotage recovery at any and all costs. For instance, in our own experiences, we saw our daughters' eating disorders take advantage of any leniency or wiggle room we allowed. Interestingly enough, it was when our daughters were progressing in their recovery that they became most susceptible to the insidious nature of their illness. As they improved physically, our daughters gradually earned back some instances of independent eating, and during these times, both of the girls refrained from eating bananas at all costs. They insisted they both hated the taste of bananas, even with cereal and milk or atop yogurt. In fact, their eating disorder had taken advantage of the fact that the girls were sensitive and anxious about the high sugar content in fruits, deeming bananas the highest of all.

If not careful, misunderstandings like this can lead to further restricting, and restricting can result in weight loss and negative energy balance, so it is important to keep in mind that wiggle room or leniency too early in recovery can be a great opportunity for "Ed" to try to take back his control.

Motivation

Expecting motivation to get better in some types of eating disorders such as anorexia nervosa, at least initially when acutely ill and malnourished, may be futile. First of all, little or no insight into his or her problem (anosognosia) is a common symptom of anorexia nervosa. Why would the individual have any motivation if he or she does not perceive that there is even a problem?

Instead, the individual is likely motivated to maintain the way he or she is and continue engaging in the eating disorder behaviors. As discussed earlier, a negative energy balance in the brain causes an individual who is predisposed to anorexia to experience the feeling of eating less (restricting or purging) as pleasant and soothing. Through starvation the individual is drawn to this antianxious state.

In the beginning, when sick and malnourished, external motivators need to be identified and employed by the individual's support team. Maybe for your loved one to please you may provide some motivation to recover; maybe it is bothersome to your loved one to see you upset, scared, angry, or worried. Perhaps receiving compliments about how strong or how hard he or she is working will drive your loved one to work in recovery. Other motivators to recover may be the option of staying out of the hospital, avoiding tube feeding, staying in school, attending college, etc. These are big-picture motivators, but as a family member supporting recovery you may need to utilize even daily measures to keep your loved one engaged and working to recover.

These measures may be the consequences you need to enforce from the expectations discussed above. Some examples may be adhering to the meal plan all week to be able to attend a high school function on the weekend, such as a sporting event or a dance; to finish dinner to be able to use the car that evening; to reach the target weight to be allowed to play on a team. You will need to develop consequences that are appropriate to your loved one.

For Jillian, I recall establishing the consequences of not allowing her to take driver's education if she could not maintain her expected weight range, and our other daughter, Amelia, would not be allowed to continue with rehearsals for the high school musical; she would be pulled from the show if she did not maintain her healthy weight range. Even when our daughters were beyond reasoning with, I still felt it necessary to explain the rationale behind these consequences. My reasoning consistently provided an explanation related to their health, such as, "if you are not nourished you cannot retain what you are being taught and you need to learn everything to become a safe driver; if you are not nourished or hydrated you could pass out while driving, get into an accident and hurt yourself and others; if you are not properly nourished you won't be able to learn your lines for the show, you won't perform your best and the cast is counting on your best, that amount of physical activity of singing and dancing will cause you to lose weight and get sicker if you are not adhering to the meal plan."

This helped to prevent these consequences from being

construed as punitive. I did not want our girls to feel as though they were being punished. Even more important, I hoped that stating the rationale for the consequences would deter our daughters from losing their interests or stunting the development of their personal, internal motivation to recover.

I can appreciate any concerns you may have that if you instill consequences that include what your loved one actually desires and enjoys, you may extinguish his or her personal motivation to recover; that taking away their favorite activity will lead them to care less and never develop his or her personal desire and motivation to recover (intrinsic motivation). Speaking from my experience, I can tell you that making and enforcing consequences (even those that interested my daughters the most) did not deter them from developing their own internal motivation to get and stay well.

Due to their altered thought processes and brain functioning from the state of starvation, your loved one will likely be irrational and unmotivated, so initially be motivated for him or her. As the individual's medical condition improves, so will the brain's ability to function properly. The things in the individual's life that excite and interest him or her will gradually become more important and drive his or her desire to recover and maintain recovery.

When Jillian was not quite at her target weight range and still unreasonable, she firmly believed she needed to regress and get sicker. She was certain she needed to get low enough to mandate hospitalization to have this whole thing "count." She thought she would have failed if she didn't require hospitalization. I know you're thinking, *that's crazy!* But these are the altered thought processes associated with this horrible sickness.

So, while she had made considerable progress she started to regress at this point. In addition to showing her some tough love or calling her bluff by arranging her admission to the hospital and having her bags packed, I finally confided in her that she was sick enough to be hospitalized. I told her that hospitalizing her was the initial recommendation, but that we made the tough decision to admit her in partial hospitalization instead, so we could keep her in school. She was a freshman and we were very concerned about the effects of being absent at this stage of her high school career. While, not what was advised, this is what we had decided. I also promised her that she felt this was important because her brain was not functioning well yet because of malnutrition; as she began to restrict again her thoughts were irrational. I promised her that when she is thirty years old, happily married, and likely a mother herself, she would not look back on this time and think she was a failure. I promised her that she would instead think back and only be proud that she worked hard and recovered. Thankfully, she has already expressed that in hindsight she is more than grateful for recovery.

Not long after hitting her target weight and maintaining, Jillian became more engaged socially and pursued with fervor her favorite activities. She started to talk about and make plans for her future; her internal motivation to get

The Enigmatic Aspects of a Mysterious Disease

and stay well developed. She found satisfaction and enjoyment in living her life again.

For Amelia, learning that self-starvation was putting her future fertility at risk was profoundly motivating to her. She very much envisioned a future with children and her desire to fulfill that dream marked a turning point in her recovery.

Initially, you may need to be motivated for your loved one. As psychologist Dr. Sarah Ravin says, "Fortunately, motivation is not necessary to begin recovery from anorexia nervosa." From some experts I have spoken with, it is not recommended that treatment (family-based or family-centered) be delayed until the individual "wants to get better" or "wants to recover." From my experience, weight restoration and stabilizing the medical condition is always the first priority. Even if they resist, which many do, because of many possible reasons, recovery must begin. Don't wait for your loved one to want to get better to start getting the help he or she needs.

When weight is restored and he or she is healthy enough to begin participating in activities, expose your loved one to the activities that interest him or her most. Seek guidance from professionals regarding the selection of appropriate activities. Immediately returning to cross-country running, for instance, will probably not be an appropriate activity early on, as I am certain you can understand. I found the participation in engaging activities effective, ones that my girls could derive pleasure and self-satisfaction, or merely enjoy. They may need some gentle nudging to reengage in their lives. Gradually, your loved one will develop his or her own personal reasons to recover and maintain recovery.

For Jillian, we enrolled her in sewing classes with a friend. It wasn't soon after starting these classes that she would make comments about wanting a career in fashion. This interest grew to a couple of internships in high school and her recent admission to business school at Miami University where she is majoring in marketing with a double minor in fashion merchandising and interactive media studies: commercialization.

During recovery when she restored her weight and was medically stable, we noticed a peak in her interest with friends and having a social life. We encouraged her in this regard, knowing this is an important part of a teenager's development and something our previously meek and anxious daughter avoided. We shouldered more driving duties than most parents and we always opened our home to her friends. As she became more social, her grades began to slip. She went from being obsessed with getting perfect grades and getting into the best college, to needing a talking to about her grades! Jillian was doing lots more with friends, going to football and hockey games, attending dances, and even had her first boyfriend. This drastic change caught me a little off guard. Her psychiatrist said to me, "she's a normal teenager now and interested in other things besides grades. For the first time you are parenting a normal teenager."

For Amelia, we supported her interest in music and theater. We encouraged her to audition for roles and enrolled her in private voice lessons. We gave her space in our home to sing to her heart's content. When busy and engaged in activities such as these, she dwelled less and less on her negative body image. These activities are enriching, rewarding, fulfilling, and simply make her happy. Gently easing her back into her favorite activities, once well enough to do so and on a limited basis, was exactly what she needed. As she progressed in recovery she expressed more and more interest in these activities as well as others. I am pleased to say that Amelia participates in a show choir and landed a lead role in her high school musical, a major highlight in her life.

What You May Never Understand

In the previous sections of this chapter, various features regarding eating disorders and what you need to understand were discussed. At this point, I wish to discuss what I call *What You May Never Understand*. This refers to numerous features of eating disorders with which you are perhaps familiar or which you may have even researched thoroughly, yet will never fully comprehend. You have enough understanding to be empathetic, but you may never completely grasp some of the following information.

For example, if you have been healthy your entire life and have never experienced loss of appetite, it may be impossible to really understand the feeling of not being hungry. Maybe you can't imagine your mind playing tricks on you or seeing something in the mirror that isn't there.

It is impossible to wrap your head around this concept of an altered body image. Sure, you may know what it feels like to feel full from having overeaten, but to compulsively binge and be out of control, or to go to the extreme measures of purging, overexercising, and/or abusing laxatives is inconceivable. However, you don't have to fully understand to be understanding. After all, you don't have an eating disorder, nor do you have all the other contributing factors, circumstances, or personal experiences of your loved one. But it is possible to be able to be empathetic, patient, and supportive. Also, remember, just as no two individuals are alike, no two eating disorders are alike. When your loved one says, "You just don't understand!" my recommendation is to agree that you don't, and you may never fully understand, but that you can "be understanding." Let her know you care, you are here for her, and that you will support recovery.

CHAPTER 5

Getting Clear on Distorted Body Image

Distorted body image may be the single most difficult aspect of an eating disorder to understand, appreciate, and support. It's important however, that no matter how complex a concept, it is legitimate. Looking in the mirror and seeing what doesn't exist is a challenging aspect for families of sufferers to grasp and a prevalent problem. Eating Disorder Hope, an organization that promotes ending eating disordered behavior states, "Body image disturbance is one of the most common clinical features attributed to eating disorders."

In your attempts to appreciate what your loved one is experiencing, take into consideration the physical and medical deterioration of an individual who is starving his or her body of nutrition. If you take into account the effects of malnutrition on his or her thought processes and mental status, then this concept of distorted body image becomes easier to comprehend. Experts refer to eating disorders as brain-based disorders; the brain is not functioning normally, but is altered.

Neuroscience research has demonstrated that brain functioning can help explain distorted body image in anorexia nervosa. With neuroimaging, researchers are identifying areas of the brain that are abnormally activated when an individual with anorexia views pictures of himself or herself (Wagner et al., 2003). Other studies reveal that the brain's fear circuitry is activated more in those suffering anorexia than in healthy subjects without an eating disorder when viewing pictures of their body that were altered to be larger (more like their normal, healthy body size and shape). Interestingly, these fear circuits were not overly activated when they viewed pictures of other individuals with healthy bodies or normal sizes and shapes (Seeger et al., 2002). These are just a sample of studies in neurobiology to support that body image distortion is real.

When your loved one views himself or herself differently than others do, how should you react? First, avoid disagreeing. Disagreeing, or even worse, arguing, is futile and likely will make matters worse as you both become frustrated and upset. Instead, I encourage you to be open and honest. Express to your loved one that you understand that the illness causes the brain to see his or her body differently than you and others do. Appreciate that distorted body image is legitimate; your loved one is not intentionally being defiant, obstinate, or difficult. Remember your loved one is suffering, and the best response is love and patience.

Getting Clear on Distorted Body Image

Being supportive includes showing empathy and compassion. Sufferers should know that you understand their struggles and that you only want to offer encouragement. Be reassuring that as they progress in recovery and the brain is functioning more normally, self-perception will get better and that means a healthier body image will follow. Stay apprised of what your loved one is learning from the professionals, so that you can be consistent and supportive at home. Request information on how to respond and how to facilitate and reinforce what is being learned in treatment. Encourage use of the skills and strategies your loved one is learning.

My daughters told me that what they appreciated from me, above anything else, was my simple acknowledgment of what they were feeling or struggling with in the moment. Instead of lecturing or trying to fix their thoughts, feelings, or struggles, I did my best to be what they said they needed from me: to just be their mom, with arms outstretched ready to hug them. That's not to say I was perfect, by any means. I did my share of lecturing, trying to fix everything, and had plenty of my own meltdowns. Although assisting them during weight restoration may have been the most valuable thing my husband and I did to support their recoveries, the one thing our daughters could not get from the team of professionals or anyone else was our love.

Even when an individual is maintaining a healthy weight range and is not malnourished, a negative body image can still exist. There are individuals who are dissatisfied with their body shape and size, but do not develop eating disorders. Negative body image is also referred to as distorted body image. It is described as "a distorted perception of your shape—you perceive parts of your body unlike they really are; you are convinced that only other people are attractive and that your body size or shape is a sign of personal failure; you feel ashamed, self-conscious, and anxious about your body; you feel uncomfortable and awkward in your body" (NEDA). From my experience with Amelia, when she was enduring altered mental status from being malnourished, her body image distortion intensified. Now, maintaining a healthy weight and having recovered in most ways, she still battles negative body image. It's not nearly as intense as it was, and fortunately she is managing these negative thoughts well with her strategies.

Interestingly, Jillian never experienced negative body image before, during, or after recovery. At the time of her illness she never expressed being unhappy with her body, and now years later and recovered, she admits she wasn't dissatisfied with her body. She actually seemed aware of her state of malnourishment and never disputed it. Based on her pretty extreme anorexia while not experiencing negative body image, I gather this aspect is not a prerequisite for the illness. Witnessing her as I did and knowing what I now know, I believe my highly anxious daughter sought the comfort of the calming, antianxiety effects of negative energy balance from self-starvation.

Remember, distorted body image is real and supported by neuroscience research as presented earlier in this chapter. Another study demonstrates just how "real" body image distortion is for those with anorexia nervosa. Individuals with anorexia that struggle with distorted body image feel fat (or larger than they actually are) on an emotional level, but also feel fat physically (Kaizer et al., 2013). Researchers found that distorted body image in anorexia leads individuals to perceive themselves as fat and unconsciously move their bodies in ways consistent with their misperceptions. "Participants walked through door-like openings varying in width while performing a diversion task" (Kaizer et al., 2013). Those with anorexia started rotating their shoulders to fit through larger openings than those without anorexia. The control group did not start rotating their shoulders until the opening was much smaller than the opening that led those with anorexia to make this perceptual adjustment. This study shows that those struggling with body distortion problems judge their bodies larger, even unconsciously, further validating just how real the distortion is for these individuals.

Eating disorders are illnesses that live in the brain. Although you may never fully understand what your loved one is experiencing, if you can appreciate that it is legitimate for your loved one, you can be supportive. When someone you love is experiencing pain (maybe from an injury, surgery, a disease), you don't feel their pain, nor do you need to in order to be compassionate for how he or she is feeling and what he or she is experiencing; you can still be supportive. The same goes for what your loved one is experiencing in regard to his or her eating disorder (such as not feeling hungry, being anxious, getting angry;

or perceiving and seeing himself or herself far different than what others do). Remain calm and patient; assist in regaining healthy eating behaviors and encourage the use of all the skills and strategies your loved one has learned. When all else fails, administer healthy dosages of love and affection, the kind of love only you can offer.

CHAPTER 6

The Eating Disordered Mind and Change in Personality

There will be no scientific research supporting this chapter. Instead, let me reassure you, based on my personal experiences as a mother witnessing two very different eating disorders, the negative changes in personality, demeanor, mood, and temperament you may witness will improve. Some experts even report that these changes represent a stage of recovery; one source identifies it as "Stage 2: anger, defiance, rebellion" (Bryant-Waugh, R. & Lask, B., 2004).

Honest personal testimony will be provided based on the two cases I witnessed, agonized over, supported, and now celebrate. Whether your child, your spouse, or close friend is struggling with an eating disorder, you may notice that this person you love, care about, and know so well is acting in a radically different manner that does not correlate to his or her previous character. Again, try to disassociate the illness from your loved one. The eating disorder may lead the individual that you know and love to say and do things far differently than he or she would normally.

Other than first being concerned about my daughters' medical condition, as I observed them both wasting away, I wondered if they would ever be themselves again. At the height of their illness, they were unrecognizable. Surely, they didn't look like themselves, but their demeanor, their disposition, their personalities were drastically different.

Amelia was always a bubbly, spirited, witty, social girl. She could entertain and amuse others so easily. She loved to laugh and make others laugh. More than anything she loved to sing. She sang anytime, anywhere. I compare her to a puppy; if the puppy isn't wagging its tail, you know something's wrong. The poor little puppy is probably scared or sick, and if our daughter wasn't singing, something was wrong. As she was losing weight, she became less engaged. She laid around the house, slept, and became depressed and uninterested in everything. She didn't want to visit with family, go to school, or be with her friends. She stopped singing. She claimed her withdrawal was all from having mononucleosis. While we were at work, however, she secretively and obsessively weighed herself, exercised, hid food, and restricted. I worried I would never see my vibrant, lively, and spunky daughter again.

As for my people-pleasing, overachieving eldest daughter, Jillian, she became ornery, mean, and hateful. She was miserable and angry, and it showed on her face, in her words, and in her voice. Everything set her off. She was completely unreasonable. My husband and I were

The Eating Disordered Mind and Change in Personality

constantly walking on eggshells around her. As her illness worsened, so did her mood. She became hurtful and mean-spirited. By the time she entered treatment, I didn't recognize my kindhearted, mild-mannered daughter. I mourned for the loss of the daughter I knew and feared I would never see again.

In hindsight, I probably should have been more concerned about the medical problems that were developing, and recognized that both of their lives were at stake. I didn't know then about the many life-threatening conditions that were already transpiring. Once we sought treatment, it was shocking and frightening to learn about the many serious physical indicators of their failing health.

If your loved one isn't his or her usual self, understand that the transformation is related to physical and psychological problems brought on by the malnutrition caused by the eating disorder. Since his or her normal disposition is masked by the illness, the individual is incapable of being who she is when in good health physically, psychologically, and emotionally. It's unrealistic to expect people to maintain their normal demeanor given everything they are going through. As with anorexia nervosa, the malnutrition alters the brain chemistry and functioning.

When trying to understand the personality changes in your loved one who is suffering from an eating disorder, consider some circumstances that may be more prevalent in life, like sleep problems or PMS. For instance, think about people who haven't been sleeping well: they stop acting like their normal selves, likely becoming easily irritable, short-tempered, lethargic, and depressed. Lack of sleep affects hormones and chemicals in the brain, similarly to how the brain is compromised when in the state of malnutrition and dehydration. Additionally, when hormones and chemicals change in the body during premenstruation, emotional changes, irritability, lethargy, and moodiness can occur. While we casually justify personality changes in these more typical circumstances, the shift and surges of hormones and chemicals affects the eating disordered brain as well. If you witness your loved one acting far different from normal, try to remember the side effects the drastic physical changes are incurring onto his or her psychological health.

Also keep in mind the similarities eating disorders have with addictions. Again, for your purposes of trying to rationalize the personality changes of your loved one, consider your loved one's irritability or other erratic emotional displays may be due, in part, to a craving. For example, those with anorexia may desire to feel calm and soothed by creating a negative energy balance by starving, therefore, when in treatment and avoiding achieving the antianxiety sensation, your loved one will likely act out.

When your loved one's medical condition is stabilized and weight is restored, the focus shifts to address underlying psychological problems. Based on my personal experiences and discussions with other caregivers, the person you care about will gradually return to his or her normal nature and demonstrate those qualities. You will gradually see your loved one's personality return. You will also

The Eating Disordered Mind and Change in Personality

see your loved one start to smile again, have opinions, and start to care about the things she used to care about. You will begin to experience more and more the person you knew before the eating disorder.

When Amelia started to sing again, it was joyous music to my ears, literally and figuratively. It was a moment I will never forget. I remember it well for a couple of reasons. When she was malnourished and depressed, it took a lot of coaxing to get her to even take a shower and maintain personal hygiene. Not only did she stop caring about how she looked, she didn't have the energy to perform this daily task. One day, after a long day spent at school and in her partial hospitalization treatment program and arriving home at nearly seven in the evening, she commented, "I'm going to take a shower." I thought to myself, *Huh, I didn't even have to plead with her.* Then next I hear her singing a One Direction song in the shower, loud enough for the neighbors to hear. I knew then we had made it. My daughter was back!

It gets even better. Your loved one will gradually return to his or her natural tendencies, his or her natural way of being, acting, thinking, and feeling. But, in many ways, your loved one may become an even better version of herself. It is said that our greatest growth comes from our adversity. This has been the case for my family. Once in treatment, you can address problems such as lack of self-confidence, need for reassurance, low self-esteem, the inability to make decisions, the need to please everyone, to overachieve, and to make comparisons to others. This is an opportunity for your loved one (and your family) to develop a sense of self-awareness, coping mechanisms, and improved communication skills. Our daughters became more capable and self-assured, accepting of themselves and developed self-love. The individual not only returns to the person he or she was before, but likely will even come back better than before, stronger and more capable. Skills are developed to handle the ups and downs of life, insecurities, and life's challenges. The personal growth in my daughters, as a result of their recovery, far exceeded anything I could have imagined. I feel they are more empowered with much personal growth and development resulting from their recoveries.

You will likely ask the professionals involved in caring for your loved one, "Will they get their personalities back?" They will reassure you that your loved one will return. I hope that hearing from a mom who simultaneously supported two daughters with eating disorders further reassures you, and I also hope this gives you one less thing to worry about while on the bumpy road to recovery.

PART II

Getting Help, Navigating Roadblocks, and Facilitating Recovery

WHAT'S INSIDE:

How to Talk About Treatment

Treatment Options

Practice, Practice, Practice

A Unified Approach

Facilitating Strategies

CHAPTER 7

How to Talk About Treatment

Perhaps you readily accept the likelihood that your loved one has an eating disorder, but he or she denies it. Or, maybe you are having trouble communicating your concerns because you have no idea what to say or how to say it. Despite how much or how little we knew about our daughters' eating disorders, there was one thing we were innately certain of: we could upset, offend, and completely shut off our girls. We know this because many of us are naturally wired to go on the defense. There are some tools and techniques that I have learned and adapted from the National Eating Disorder Association (NEDA TOOLKIT for Parents) that may mitigate some of the fear you have of engaging in what can quickly become a heated argument, or worse, a trigger for more eating disordered behavior.

When broaching the subject of getting treatment, it is critical to have already lined up, or investigated, professional help. Encouraging your loved one to seek treatment may be the single most important thing you can do to help. Here are a few recommendations adapted from the National Eating Disorder Association on how to talk in a way so that your loved one will hear you.

- **Rehearse what you want to say or write out your main points.**

  Your emotions will be running high, but you don't want to be led by them when starting this conversation. Instead, talk about behaviors and changes you have observed and calmly point out why you are concerned. You can accomplish this by employing specific statements and directly but sincerely stating, "I have seen you run to the bathroom after meals and that makes me worried you might be making yourself throw up," or "I see you packing less and less in your lunches, and I am concerned you aren't getting what you need to have good energy and do well in school."

- **While it may be clear to you that the person has a problem and needs help, it may not be as clear to your loved one.**

  Empathize with how he or she may be feeling (maybe ashamed, scared, or anxious). Anosognosia (a lack of insight or self-awareness) is a common symptom of eating disorders and understandable in those who are malnourished.

- **Be prepared for negative reactions.**
  Individuals suffering from an eating disorder may be resistant and deny they have a problem. Becoming angry is a common response to your concern. Again, lack of insight/awareness is a common symptom of this illness that lives in the brain.

- **Avoid making statements that place blame or guilt.**
  Sounding accusatory by asserting, "You just need to eat"; "Just stop"; "You're not eating upsets me so much"; or "You're exercising too much" needs to avoided. Not only do these comments place blame, they are overly simplistic, which may leave your loved one feeling frustrated, defensive, and misunderstood. Instead use "I" statements. Focus on behaviors that you have personally observed. For instance, "*I* have noticed that you aren't eating dinner with us anymore," or "*I* am worried how frequently you are going to the gym." Sounding accusatory can happen as a result of your frustration and desperation. Preparing for these conversations may help you remain calm and phrase your concerns rationally instead of emotionally.

- **Eating disorder sufferers may be hesitant to change their behaviors.**
  If your loved one proves resistant, consider focusing on the side effects that you may be noticing such

as depression, anxiety, insomnia, fatigue, weakness, feeling cold, loss of menstruation, or hair loss. You may want to gently bring up real and serious medical complications that may result, such as infertility, kidney damage, loss of bone density, heart damage, or death.

- **Present reasons for getting well.**

    One day having children, going to college, participation in certain activities, or having a certain career can all be motivators for recovery.

- **Don't buy the eating disorder's excuses.**

    An eating disorder is clever. Remember resistance toward getting help is likely.

- **Offer to make the call and to accompany the individual to the appointment.**

    This will help your loved one feel supported and not alone. He or she will also get a sense of the seriousness of the illness and of the importance of getting help; the message is that this cannot be ignored or postponed.

- **Remove potential stigma.**

    Remind your loved one that there is no shame in admitting to struggling with an eating disorder. Explain the reality that many people suffer from eating disorders and other mental health problems, and that they can recover.

How to Talk About Treatment

- **Remind your loved one that their life will be waiting for them after treatment.** The person suffering with the eating disorder may become upset by the thought that treatment will mean missing school, college, work, or a certain activity. When making decisions about treatment, recovery comes first. Everything else can wait. Explain that if your loved one had a broken leg, of course, they would seek medical help.

If your loved one denies having a problem, NEDA suggests, "What you need to do as a parent won't necessarily depend on your child's ability to believe there is something wrong." In other words, if you are dealing with a minor, you are still in charge. Regardless of whether the person suffering from an eating disorder is a child or an adult, the specialists are experienced at working with individuals who do deny or are unaware of their problem. Therefore, "Get them in the door," urges NEDA, "where the eating disorder can begin to be addressed."

In short, your child does not have to admit to or acknowledge her behavior in order to benefit from getting help.

However, an intervention like this gets much more difficult when individuals are over the age of eighteen. In these circumstances, NEDA suggests using "whatever leverage you have." For instance, if you are providing any financial assistance to them, have that assistance contingent on seeking treatment. If living with your child, NEDA suggests setting boundaries regarding what behaviors you will accept in your home. As an example, NEDA explains that you set boundaries no differently than boundaries for other things such as no drugs. While your child is a minor, maybe your rule is no driving with other kids you don't know, no boys in the house alone . . . While you would probably change those issues for the one you face right now, setting boundaries on eating disordered behavior is no different. As easily as you would demand the child abstain from any potentially unsafe and harmful activity, the same could be said for an eating disordered behavior. You are basically setting expectations and consequences so you can "calmly, clearly, and consistently follow through."

My husband and I set numerous expectations along the way and used leverage like driver's education, attending a school dance, driving the car, and considering visiting out-of-state colleges for campus tours. The paradox with this approach is that usually by advanced stages of eating disorders, sufferers have become withdrawn and have lost interest in the things they care about, making leveraging such things a bit tricky. But, if you dig deep enough, you will find something, anything, even the least likely thing, to use in order to ignite the spark of motivation. Start small and slow. It doesn't have to be something as threatening as, say, pulling your son from the wrestling team, especially if he is too weak to even attend workouts. But it can be something that communicates you are not trusting him the way you used to, such as no longer allowing him to babysit his younger sibling because you think he is not strong enough to do it. Until he starts feeding himself, you can't trust him as a caregiver for an innocent child. Such a statement can be a motivator.

Such strategies are used to communicate to individuals that their behaviors are detrimental and that they have a problem, need help, and must practice healthy eating behaviors. While NEDA presents these recommendations in their TOOLKIT for Parents on their website, https://www.nationaleatingdisorders.org/parent-toolkit, it seems reasonable that these would be effective in adult relationships as well (such as with a spouse). "The expectation that they will receive treatment and recover from their disorder is powerful medicine for a sufferer," contends NEDA.

Sufferers of eating disorders become extremely despondent, so they may not believe recovery is possible, but knowing that their family and friends *expect* recovery makes it *feel* possible.

In circumstances where the eating disorder has gone unchecked for a long time, as mentioned earlier, leveraging through the use of consequences or setting expectations may not work, as long-time sufferers with extremely affected brain chemistry likely lose interest in the activities they used to care about. So, while taking away an extracurricular activity or not allowing a slumber party may have worked before, your loved one might not be motivated by the loss of these things. Depression, isolation, shame, and fatigue plague people with eating disorders, and their preference is to retreat. If this is the case for you, and your consequences and expectations are ineffective, take NEDA's advice, and get your loved one through the door of a treatment center and allow professionals to intervene (this includes initiating Family-Based Treatment at home or Family-Centered Treatment in a clinic or facility).

CHAPTER 8

Treatment Options

The moment we accepted the realities and decided Jillian needed help (which was followed only minutes later by Amelia voluntarily admitting she, too, had a problem), I picked up the telephone and called the mental health hospital located in the city in which we live. I knew this facility's eating disorder programs were highly respected, not only in this country, but across the world. We felt fortunate to have this hospital in our backyard. Many individuals and families often need to travel and relocate to receive treatment (which only adds to the costs and stress associated with receiving care). I was aware that this hospital provided different levels of care and used a family-centered approach. My husband and I very much wanted to be actively involved in their recoveries. To us, this was the obvious next step.

What we didn't know then was that there is another treatment approach called Family-Based Treatment (FBT), also called the Maudsley approach. FBT is an effective treatment option of adolescent anorexia nervosa (and I understand it is effective with treating adolescent bulimia nervosa). Having two daughters (our only two children) both battling anorexia simultaneously may have made FBT more challenging, or maybe all together easier. I am not sure, and fortunately we have no regrets as the Family-Centered approach and programming that we used was effective.

I am not promoting one treatment approach over another. Individuals and families may need to take many factors into consideration when deciding on the right treatment. Some of those factors may include the medical condition of the individual, health insurance coverage, availability of a hospital or clinic in your area, ability to travel if needed, availability of caregivers and/or their ability to take off from work as necessary, costs associated with care, family circumstances, and the needs of other family members. In this chapter, I offer a simplified overview of both approaches—Family-Based Treatment and Family-Centered Treatment.

Family-Based Treatment (FBT)

Originally called the Maudsley approach because it was developed at the Maudsley Hospital in London, England, in the 1970s, this is an intensive refeeding approach with parents as key participants in the refeeding of their child. It is a treatment approach for adolescents with anorexia nervosa to prevent hospitalization, and is described as an "intensive outpatient treatment where parents play an

Treatment Options

active and positive role" (Maudsleyparents.org). It is a treatment method recommended for children and adolescents and for those with recent versus chronic eating disorders. The treatment involves three phases: 1) weight restoration, 2) returning control of eating to the adolescent, and 3) establishing a healthy adolescent identity.

Parents are given the challenging task of ensuring the adolescent takes in adequate nutrition to restore his or her weight. Parents and adolescents can seek support and coaching of a therapist with specialized training in FBT. The therapist supports the parents and other family members in their feeding efforts and helps parents/family to understand the adolescent is not to be blamed: that the illness is separate from their child.

Central to this approach are the fundamental principles that the adolescent and his or her family are not the cause of the eating disorder. The other principle is that the adolescent is not in control of his or her eating disordered behaviors, but rather the illness is in control. This is especially important if the adolescent resists eating; it's the illness of anorexia nervosa that resists eating, not the adolescent. Understanding this also empowers parents in taking a strong stand against the eating disorder. Although the adolescent may resist eating, become angry, or exhibit any number of behaviors out of fear or anxiety, when this treatment approach is effective, eventually the adolescent (or I should say the illness) surrenders more and more to his or her parents taking charge of what is necessary to reach or maintain a healthy weight. The FBT approach is described to involve "compassionate, yet persistent and firm expectations that your adolescent eat an amount of food that can reverse the state of starvation his or her body is in" (Maudsleyparents.org). "Parents learn to stay calm in the face of an adolescent's anxiety attacks and angry outbursts, supporting them through meals including foods they fear" (Muhlheim, 2016).

FBT is deemed an effective treatment. Studies report that 67 percent of adolescents are recovered at the end of FBT, and after five years, 75–90 percent had restored their weight (maudsleyparents.org). More recently, research at the University of Chicago and Stanford University demonstrates that adolescents usually require less than twenty FBT sessions over a period of six to twelve months, and at that time 80 percent were weight restored and resumed menstruation (maudsleyparents.org).

Family-Centered Treatment

Treatment provided by trained professionals or a team of professionals in a hospital, clinic, or office will be described next. This approach is individualized and may use a Family-Centered Therapy approach (FCT). There are different levels of treatment and treatment settings available. The National Eating Disorders Association TOOLKIT for Parents provides a thorough resource that includes additional details about treatment information, including an American Psychiatric Association chart, which specifies guidelines for professionals in determining and recommending the appropriate level of care (NEDA, 2015).

Treatment Options

When the healthcare provider or program is determining its recommendation for level of care or treatment setting (full hospitalization, partial hospitalization, outpatient, or family-based therapy), the following factors are considered:

- The individual's medical status
- Weight
- Motivation to recover
- The individual's insight into the problem
- Co-occurring problems (such anxiety or depression)
- Suicide risk
- Amount of supervision needed to eat or not to restrict, purge, compulsively exercise, or binge
- The individual's home environment (supportive family/friends, or an environment that either lacks family/friends for support or family/friends are unable to provide the level of support needed)
- The availability of treatment programs in the individual's geographic area

Insurance coverage or treatment costs may also contribute to decisions made regarding treatment selection. Most providers will establish insurance preauthorization for treatment. Medical examination or medical tests may be necessary prior to obtaining treatment recommendations and admission into treatment.

Eating disorder treatment may be provided in an acute care hospital, in a residential treatment center, or in a clinic or office setting. Individuals may enter treatment at any level of care and move to a greater or lesser level of care depending on the course of their individual recovery. Usually (because of limited resources) the plan is to provide treatment in the least restrictive or intense setting that will be effective. Some may start in outpatient and progress to a higher level of care, while some (maybe because illness was not identified until it progressed in severity) start in a hospital or residential treatment and then graduate to lesser levels of care. Ideally, individuals are dropped down in a stepwise fashion. Depending on an individual's needs (at any point in recovery), treatment may consist of one, all, or a combination of the following: medical care and monitoring, nutritional care and counseling, psychotherapy (individual, group, and/or family), and medication treatment (such as antianxiety medication).

Cognitive behavioral therapy (CBT) is a psychotherapy often used in the treatment of eating disorders. According to Dr. Lauren Muhlheim and her colleagues at Eating Disorder Therapy LA, CBT is "a treatment based on the idea that how one thinks (cognition), feels (emotion), and behaves (behavior) all interact together . . . one's thoughts determine one's feelings and behavior." She adds, "CBT helps to change the way you think, feel, and behave."

Initially, the individual's medical condition is top

priority. To medically stabilize the individual, the first focus is to restore the individual to a healthy weight. When restoring and maintaining weight, meal plans are a key component in treatment. Meal plans provide structure and organization to the amount and types of foods needed throughout recovery. These meal plans are to be adhered to inside and outside of treatment (such as at home, work, or school). Modifications (usually by a dietician) are made as necessary in order to gain and to maintain weight. The eventual goal is to wean the individual from needing a meal plan. When the individual is ready, increased independence is gradually returned so the individual may regain "intuitive eating." The five treatment categories and settings for eating disorders are as follows.

Level V: Inpatient Treatment

This level of care has the primary focus of stabilizing the patient's medical condition with medical monitoring and care, structure, and supervision to prevent restricting, purging, overexercising, or bingeing. Once medically stable, the individual is discharged to the next appropriate level of care (residential, partial hospitalization, intensive outpatient, or outpatient treatment), where the focus of care shifts to addressing psychological problems, obsessive thoughts, and/or compulsive behaviors.

Level IV: Residential Treatment

The individual resides at a treatment facility. This type of treatment differs from hospitalization or inpatient treatment, as the goal for this level of care is not to stabilize the individual's medical condition but rather to focus on the individual's psychological issues. The individual is in need of constant structure and supervision to address and prevent compulsive behaviors of restricting, purging, overexercising, or bingeing and to continue weight restoration if needed.

Level III: Partial Hospitalization

Partial hospitalization is treatment where the individual lives at home and attends treatment for part or most of the day. The duration of the treatment may vary from a few hours per day to all day, depending on the facility or program and may depend on individual needs as well. Medical monitoring may be provided at this level of care with a nurse as part of the treatment team. The individual needs structure and supervision for most of his or her meals at this level of care. Individual and group psychotherapy, education on numerous topics related to eating disorders and recovery, nutritional counseling, nursing assessments, psychiatric care, art therapy, outings with food challenges, and family therapy may be included in partial hospitalization.

Our daughters began their eating disorder recovery treatment in a partial hospitalization program. They attended school in the morning and arrived to their program at 11:30 a.m. and were in treatment until 6:00 p.m., five days a week. They were supervised during lunch, one afternoon snack, and dinner on each of these days. Their program included all of the above features. Each partial hospitalization program will have its own specific schedule, hours of operation, and number of days per week.

Level II: Intensive Outpatient

Intensive outpatient consists of more regularly scheduled time in treatment and will likely include individual and group treatment, nutritional counseling, meal supervision, and family counseling. These programs may occur during the day or in the evening; they fit between needing the intensity of partial hospitalization and the less intense outpatient treatment.

Our experience with intensive outpatient occurred after Jillian was discharged from partial hospitalization. This intensive outpatient program was scheduled for three mandatory and specified days per week (4 to 7 p.m.). All of the abovementioned features were part of this program. The families joined the group one evening per week for the last two hours to share an evening meal and family group session. This program provided an effective transition from partial hospitalization. Being involved in the program one evening per week provided us, her parents, with valuable information regarding expectations, strategies, and further education.

Level I: Outpatient

Outpatient treatment is provided usually as individual sessions with various members of the treatment team, such as the psychiatrist, psychotherapist, and dietician. The frequency of sessions will vary depending on many factors and will be recommended by the professional with input from the individual and family. In general, it is expected that more frequent treatment sessions will be needed initially, and as the individual progresses, the frequency of treatment sessions decreases. However, recovery does not always take a straight course. Sometimes it may seem that your loved one takes a few steps forward and one giant step back. It's important, as the support system, to focus on the positives and the overall improvement. There may be times when the individual needs more frequent outpatient treatment sessions, for any number of possible reasons. As he or she is living life outside of treatment (going to school or to work, living and spending time with family/friends, socializing, participating in activities . . .), issues and challenges may arise. This may entail increasing frequency of treatment sessions to temporarily assist the individual in overcoming and managing challenges.

Be prepared that outpatient treatment for your loved one will take its own course and a change in frequency of treatment sessions may occur. It may not be a course that tapers off perfectly and gradually. There may be a few hurdles to overcome along the way that will require a change.

If your loved one is being treated with medications for anxiety or depression, expect routine visits with the prescribing physician (likely a psychiatrist). Medication treatment will need monitoring by the ordering physician and may need adjustments.

Seeking treatment by providers that specialize in eating disorders is highly recommended. However, doing so may require travel, depending on your geographical area and availability of eating disorder professional. Online and telephone service delivery options are available for individuals needing this form of treatment.

Jillian began outpatient treatment with a psychotherapist specializing in anxiety and obsessive-compulsive disorders (OCD). While this therapist was well-qualified in treating anxiety, she was not as qualified in identifying eating disorders; initially valuable time was spent focusing only on Jillian's anxiety. What Jillian really needed was to have her eating disorder identified and treated, which would include addressing her underlying anxiety. Not identifying (or in my case, not admitting to myself that my daughter was also struggling with an eating disorder) only led her to further physical deterioration. Fortunately, I followed my instincts and the concerns of others, and eventually sought specialized treatment for eating disorders. Once her medical condition was stabilized in a partial hospitalization program providing Family-Centered Treatment, the eating disorder program provided psychotherapy for her anxiety disorder.

Telemedicine, telephone therapy, email, the internet, computer software, CD-ROMs, and virtual reality are also available for individuals when direct face to-face involvement of a therapist (or team of professionals) is not possible. These reasons may include limitations of insurance coverage or lack thereof, treatment costs, or availability in a certain geographic area and inability to travel for care.

YOUR TREATMENT PLAN

While navigating the various treatment options for your loved one, please don't forget to care for yourself. This is a long and arduous road, and you won't be any good or any help to your loved one if you burn out and let stress get the best of you. I know it's easier said than done, and it is tempting to just keep going to avoid collapsing, but you must take steps to manage your own anxiety and stress levels. Being less stressed will make you more capable of being patient, understanding, and empathic—all key to providing optimal support. Open communication with the treatment team (which you should consider yourself an integral part of) is vital for effective treatment. Don't keep concerns to yourself for whatever reason. Holding back your private fears will be a negative distraction and lead to your feeling more overwhelmed. Once you address a concern, you will feel reassured that it is common, that the team has experience with it and has answers and recommendations. Feeling reassured and hopeful will in turn lead you to remain positive and encouraging toward your loved one. You will also feel empowered and confident to adhere to the recommendations and at times take some strong stands with your loved one, in an effort to support recovery. I can't stress enough, seek answers to your questions and raise your concerns in a timely manner.

Just the Stats

The following are some interesting statistics and information on the effectiveness of treatment on eating disorder recovery:

- The earlier treatment is provided the better the chances for recovery (Farrar, Tabitha, 2014).

- One in ten individuals suffering with an eating disorder receives treatment (Farrar, Tabitha, 2014).

- Eighty percent of those who receive professional treatment for their eating disorder either fully recover or make significant progress (Strober, 1997).

CHAPTER 9

Practice, Practice, Practice

Practice makes perfect. We've all heard this expression. We know practice is essential to becoming really good at doing something. Think of things you and others have practiced and spent countless hours doing to get really good at (playing baseball, singing, learning a dance routine, perfecting crème Brule, giving a presentation); they have all required much time and effort.

Sometimes we practice so much that we develop blisters and calluses. Therefore, when it comes to something as instinctive as eating, if we practice it a certain way, over and over, we get really good at doing it in that way. Maybe it becomes habitual in nature, and we know how hard habits are to break. Quitting bad habits, such as smoking cigarettes, biting our fingernails, cracking our knuckles, can all be real challenges, and many times we are unaware we are even doing them. Ask anyone who has tried to quit smoking or avoid coffee. Thinking about eating disorder behaviors in this way (in addition to the positive sensations from their negative energy balance and the similarities with addictions) helped me to appreciate how difficult it was for my daughters to discontinue the harmful eating disordered behaviors (such as restricting). Please allow me to be perfectly clear, I am not suggesting that the multifaceted, complex mental illnesses of an eating disorder is as simple as a bad habit because they aren't. But with such an elusive illness, I have found it helpful to find any aspect of it that I can relate to, and this relatability may help you keep your patience, empathy, and supportiveness that can make a difference in your loved one's recovery. Whatever your loved one's eating disordered behaviors are, likely she has only gotten better at them the longer she has been doing them. This further supports the recommendation for early and aggressive treatment to improve the chances of a full recovery.

In treatment at any level, whether in an outpatient treatment program, in an intensive outpatient program (where a few meals every week are eaten), partial hospitalization (where more meals are eaten in treatment than at home), or in an inpatient or residential program (where all meals are eaten in the hospital or treatment), or at home with family in Family-Based Therapy (FBT), the goal remains the same at every meal: to practice healthy eating behaviors and eliminate the eating disordered behaviors. The short-term goal is to achieve this with supervision and assistance, while the long-term goal is to continue and maintain the use of healthy eating behaviors independently. Achieving this goal takes time and depends on many factors, such as self-awareness, coexisting problems, motivation, medical condition, and length of time the eating disorder behaviors have been practiced.

The person suffering from an eating disorder may resist and/or have no motivation to extinguish his or her eating disorder behaviors. Remember these eating disordered behaviors are what the individual knows, what he or she has relied on. To further complicate matters, the individual may have no awareness that he or she even has a problem (anosgnosia). With anorexia nervosa, the effects of negative energy balance leading the individual to receive positive biofeedback (a calming effect) only further perpetuates the problem. This resistance may present the greatest challenge in recovery.

In your efforts to support a full recovery it's important to understand the need for developing consistent expectations, consistent strategies, consistent encouragement, and consistent responses to the individual's resistance. Your loved one must know that what is expected at meals while in treatment is going to be followed at home with parents, spouses, or other caregivers. Practicing good communication is essential among the team of professionals and the family. I encourage you to even request the exact wording the team uses in treatment for addressing certain issues. Knowing the terminology will be effective for many reasons. Your loved one will make the connection that there is communication going on between you and the treatment team. Knowledge that communication is occurring between you and the treatment team will hopefully deter the individual from attempting to revert to his or her eating disordered behaviors while at home, work, or school. Hearing the consistent messages, instructions, expectations, and words of encouragement can be extremely effective. In Family-Based Treatment, caregivers need to practice consistency and follow through on consequences. Although this may be difficult during an emotionally charged and stressful time, consistency sends a powerful message and is highly effective in making the changes necessary (including the cessation of eating disordered behaviors and a person's negative responses to expectations).

Initially, our daughters were both participating in a partial hospitalization program. This program entailed eating lunch, a snack, and dinner in the program five times a week. At home over the weekends, the girls attempted to restrict at breakfast. I placed many calls to the dietician or to their respective therapist reporting their behavior. When they arrived for treatment, the team addressed my daughters' noncompliance. The eating disorder's power and control were being taken away, thanks to our tag-team approach. We were a united front—not against our daughters, but against their disease. I mentioned earlier in this book the idea of separating the disease from the person, which was an approach that bestselling author Jenni Schaefer learned in her own treatment. As she discusses in her book *Life Without Ed: How One Woman Declared Independence from Her Eating Disorder and How You Can Too,* Jenni was taught by her therapist to treat her eating disorder as a relationship, not a condition. Similarly, we could teach our daughters to fight against their disease,

Practice, Practice, Practice

and empower themselves each time they stared in the face of their disease and achieved even the smallest triumph, beginning with compliance. If they didn't want to comply, we could discuss that it wasn't my girls' choosing to be sick, but their disease wanting that for them.

To prevent noncompliance over future weekends, we openly discussed our concerns in our family sessions with our daughters, the psychiatrist, therapists, and dietician. We learned the skills needed to stand up to the eating disorder, the illness, and not blame our daughters. All involved in the care of our daughters presented a united front because we learned to perceive the eating disorder as a separate entity that will find whatever wiggle room it can in order to get its way. Our daughters learned in treatment "Noncompliance is *not* an option" and that when they felt tempted to regress, to recognize their disease as the culprit and push back with healthy choices and thoughts. We repeated and reinforced this instruction at home.

Our daughters needed consistent messages and expectations to *practice* healthy eating behaviors. This approach was highly effective and I believe crucial to the success of their recovery. I also firmly believe the consistency and reinforcement we practiced also accounts for the relatively short period of time it took for our girls to adhere to their respective meal plans and discontinue their eating disordered behaviors. This doesn't mean we didn't experience our share of clever attempts to resist along with meltdowns, because we certainly did, but these negative responses to our expectations ended sooner than I imagined.

Recovery is not as easy as "just stop" the behavior or thought or "just eat." Eating disorder behaviors are insidious and secretive and usually have had time to become ingrained and habitual. Much practice and supervision will be needed to develop healthy eating behaviors and reverse the damaging processes the person has become dependent upon. Practice may need to occur in treatment with skilled professionals to train, educate, and facilitate the development and use of the healthy eating behaviors. Parents, spouses, or other family members may need coaching and assistance in developing their skills to stand up to the eating disorder with compassion and to effectively supervise meals at home, work, or school.

CHAPTER 10

A Unified Approach

Surprisingly, when I referred to "the meal plan" (as established in their Family-Centered Therapy), my daughters were quick to discontinue their challenges against what we expected them to consume at home. Both of our girls responded well to this structure, to their meal plans.

The literature discusses the same in FBT, as the first stage of recovery prioritizes weight restoration. As parents take the responsibility of deciding what and how much food needs to be consumed, the individual responds well to the structure and that someone else has control over the eating related decisions. This structure likely alleviates the individual of this burden that the eating disorder has imparted.

Turn to the therapist in FBT or the treatment team in FCT for suggestions on ways to set and enforce expectations. Ask for assistance in handling push back and negative responses.

"Noncompliance is *not* an option." We heard the

psychiatrist use that phrase in one of our weekly family sessions as she encouraged our girls to follow the meal plan (the expectations) while at home over the weekend. When our girls were struggling over the weekend, I would simply state that phrase, or ask the girls, "What does Dr. C say?" They could easily restate this simple, but powerful message. Having me use this phrase and expectation worked exceedingly well. We were unified. Borrowing this statement armed us with some effective phrasing. I remember using that phrase as actually being one of the first times I expressed an expectation about eating that did not have frustration or anger attached. I witnessed the psychiatrist deliver this expectation firmly, but without it coming across as punitive. Instead, it was clear, genuine, and encouraging. Most interestingly to me was that this statement and the way in which it was delivered also did not diminish how difficult this task would likely be for our daughters. It came across as motivational, that they could achieve this, yet it was empathetic of what our girls were struggling with and experiencing.

If your loved one is eating meals at school or work (this may depend on many variables, including the stage of recovery), you may need to address the issue of meal compliance and preventing use of eating disorder behaviors in these environments. Consult with the therapist or treatment team for suggestions. I have heard many ideas to assure continued progress occurs, including having your loved one be excused for snacks and lunch to have the supervision needed or designating a coworker or guidance counselor to supervise. Devise a plan that meets your loved one's situation, needs, and stage of recovery. Remember that this should match where your loved one is now, with gradual independence given back to your loved one as appropriate.

The idea of a unified approach extends beyond just compliance with eating behaviors and includes the strategies and skills the individual is developing in treatment (such as decision making, body checking, thought challenges, thought replacement, antianxiety breathing). Learn what he or she is learning. Learn the phrasing that is used in treatment to facilitate use of these strategies and skills outside of treatment for carryover to his or her personal life and to improve independence with these strategies and skills.

Communicate and work together as family and friends with the therapist and/or treatment team. Turn to each other for support and suggestions. Collaborative efforts are far more effective in supporting your loved one to a full recovery.

I hope these explanations and examples help you to recognize and appreciate the importance of having a unified approach from the start. Consistent messages regarding the expectations will assist your loved one in carrying over what he or she is accomplishing in treatment to his or her personal life outside of therapy.

As parents, we strive to address issues regarding our children as a unified front. When we are disciplining, we should agree on the consequence and support the decision, together. If we decide to ground a child, one parent can't undermine the decision, be a pushover, be manipulated by the teen, and let him or her go out with friends behind the other parent's back. Or, let's say a teen is being disrespectful to one or both parents. The parents discuss and set a reasonable expectation and explain it to the teen. Perhaps we tell them, "Okay we understand there will be times when you are in a bad mood or irritable. That's understandable, but being disrespectful is not acceptable. Let us know you are in a bad mood and we will give you some space." This is an agreed upon expectation. Going forward, one parent can't then give every excuse justifying the teen's disrespect in the presence of the teenager, by asserting, "Oh, he had a bad day" or "she has her period." What happens as a result? The teenager gets mixed messages. He or she doesn't understand that there really are expectations and consequences that will be enforced. This dynamic shouldn't stop because of the eating disorder, but should be applied to the eating disorder recovery.

Setting expectations and consequences is necessary when supporting recovery. This does not suggest you should be punitive; instead remaining loving and compassionate is recommended. Be unified with the other members of his or her support system, the treatment team, or FBT therapist. Remember the eating disorder is clever and wants control. The person suffering likely will resist at times to appease the eating disorder. You need to work collaboratively. The individual may try to get away with certain behaviors with "so and so" because he or she is

A Unified Approach

perceived as a pushover, "so and so" knows I will get angry if he or she tells on me, or "so and so" can't handle it if I get upset. If you give an inch on any expectations, the eating disorder will take a mile (or much more).

When our daughters were in partial hospitalization, eating two meals, five days a week in treatment, we were encouraged to eat with them at the evening meal. I was shocked to witness my daughters and the rest of the group all adhering to the expectations without any resistance. They were expected to eat and drink everything at the meal. They were expected to bring their tray to the supervising therapist to verify they ate and drank everything. They stood there holding their tray while the therapist lifted, shook, and checked to ensure everything was consumed. At first I thought, *how humiliating!*, but those in the group readily accepted these expectations.

I learned later that such supervision and expectations are indeed necessary to extinguish the compulsive behaviors. The takeaway here for us, as the support system, is to establish expectations and to be consistent. This approach can be achieved calmly, with love and compassion, and should never be punitive. But to be effective, the expectations need to be expressed clearly and upheld.

How do we accomplish this, when we are walking on eggshells already? Remember to separate your loved one from the illness. Do your best to stay calm. Hold firm in your expectations. Again, stand up to the eating disorder, not your loved one. Expect push back and for your loved one to become upset and angry. Remember, he or she has likely come to find solace and stress relief through his or her self-starvation or bingeing, so it will be hard for your loved one to agree to the expectations. But, if you are prepared ahead of time of what to expect and how you will respond, you will likely be able to refrain from an emotional response yourself. Remain consistent and eventually the eating disorder will retreat and have less and less control. Sooner or later, your loved one will be able to comply with the expectations without negative emotional responses. Recovery is not a sprint, it's a marathon that requires lots of patience.

CHAPTER 11

Facilitating Strategies

Individuals with eating disorders need you to advocate and help them seek professional help. But they need many other things, too. They need your nonjudgmental, emotional support, and encouragement throughout recovery. They need your unconditional love, your compassion, and your empathy. They need your strength and unwavering commitment to recovery. When sufferers do not believe they can overcome this illness, that's when they need reassurance the most. Above all, they need you to champion them on the road to recovery.

During one of our family sessions, I was struck by something one of the therapists impressed on my younger daughter. She informed my daughter that more than any therapy or any medication, the best thing for overall emotional and psychological well-being is good nutrition, good sleep, and regular exercise.

This advice is so simple yet so profound. In my opinion, these aspects of our lives are too often overlooked. In these busy, hectic times we live in, it seems we don't do these three things consistently well. If one or more are off, we certainly feel it. But, when we do them, we recognize the benefits. We underestimate the effects of these three simple aspects of self-care. Think about how you feel if you haven't been sleeping well, or if you have been so busy that you haven't been eating properly or regularly. You are likely to become irritable and cranky. Your energy level is low. Now think about how you feel after regular exercise. You sleep better. Your energy level is higher. Your mood is better. These three simple lifestyle habits combat stress. Research continues to confirm the benefits of this.

We all benefit from having balance in our lives. If an individual battling an eating disorder has coexisting problems of depression or anxiety just learning about and practicing these three simple habits for physical and emotional health may provide enormous benefits. It is important to know that exercise will most likely be limited during recovery until weight is fully restored. Follow the instructions and recommendations from the treatment team as to when and how much physical activity is recommended at various points along recovery. Also, caution must be observed to the potential threat of overexercising and development of this as a compulsive behavior. It is imperative that you seek direction from the eating disorder professionals regarding exercise and adhere closely to their recommendations. Discussions about the purpose of exercise and physical activity are important. With anorexia and bulimia, exercise needs to be for our physical and emotional health, not for weight loss. You may need to supervise and monitor exercise or any physical activity to prevent the eating disorder from creeping into these activities. It should also be noted that these lifestyle habits for emotional health are not a substitute for treatment. An individual demonstrating signs or symptoms of an eating disorder needs professional help. These healthy habits should be used to complement and support treatment; they represent universal lifestyle habits for long-term physical and emotional well-being.

The lifestyle habits above were discussed with my oldest daughter when she was experiencing sleeping difficulties, which is not unusual for those suffering with eating disorders. Recommendations were made to help her get enough quality sleep during recovery and beyond. She needed sleep to help her benefit from the work she was doing in treatment. Proper rest would help to stabilize her emotions and manage her coexisting anxiety problems.

Facilitating these three lifestyle habits are important for emotional health during recovery but are also vitally important throughout a person's lifetime. For our daughters, this was important to learn for recovery and to maintain recovery. Establishing proper nutrition and hydration is the initial focus, emphasized throughout treatment. Maintaining it is ingrained in treatment as being essential for emotional and physical well-being. Pay attention to how much sleep your loved one is getting and discuss the quality of his or her sleep. If they are not getting adequate rest, discuss this with the care provider.

Now, let's move on to treatment and your involvement in assisting your loved one. The most effective professional treatment for eating disorders is highly individualized. It involves medical and nutritional intervention along with psychotherapy or counseling (National Eating Disorders Association, 2007). The psychotherapy most often used for eating disorders is Cognitive-Behavioral Treatment (CBT). There are professionals, clinics, programs, and hospitals that specialize in eating disorders throughout the country and the world. More information about the different options and settings for treatment was discussed in Chapter 8: Treatment Options, including information on another treatment approach for adolescents with anorexia or bulimia called Family-Based Therapy (FBT).

In treatment, the individual will participate in numerous activities as part of his or her psychotherapy or counseling to address psychological problems (such as anxiety, low self-esteem, distorted body image, or perfectionism). Ongoing education will be provided on numerous topics (such as eating disorders, healthy behaviors, nutritional information, and potential health consequences resulting from eating disorders). Coping skills, strategies, self-awareness, and communication skills will be established that are effective for the individual. There are many interventions and aspects of treatment, but this book is not an eating disorder treatment book. The professionals working with your loved one will provide them with the care needed to get well. The professionals will also prepare and assist you as the support system.

FACILITATING STRATEGIES

As I've emphasized before, I strongly suggest that you maintain regular communication with those working with your loved one. Learn what your loved one is learning so you're at least familiar with the concepts. Ask how you can support these aspects outside of treatment. You may need further explanations and examples beyond what your family member relays to you or is able to explain. You may benefit from practicing the strategies and skills with the therapist yourself to obtain a deeper understanding of the concepts, strategies, and skills. This type of understanding, once again, requires good communication between family, therapist, or treatment team. The professionals have a wealth of knowledge and ideas, and the family should take full advantage of their expertise and experience.

For example, Amelia worked on "thought challenging" (a strategy by which we recognize that thoughts are just thoughts, not necessarily accurate, and so we question the thought.) Initially, the concept made sense to me, but when I attempted to practice it with my daughter I had a lot of difficulty challenging a thought myself or assisting her in formulating a challenge. Therefore, I wasn't helpful facilitating the use of that strategy. I asked for concrete examples to help me better understand how to challenge a thought and then practiced the strategy with her therapist. While I didn't give my daughter challenges to her negative and eating disorder thoughts, by understanding the strategy I was better able to coach her to formulate her own challenges to her thoughts. Usually, my role was to prompt her by saying, *What strategy could you use to help yourself?* Or *Okay now challenge that thought.*

Jillian tended to catastrophize her thoughts. During a session with her, I observed and learned the technique of asking what evidence she had to support such thoughts. I could use these prompts at home when she experienced or expressed those types of thoughts to promote her application of this strategy.

For instance, Jillian, my perfectionist, worried about things like, "If I don't get an A on this test, my grade point average will go down... I won't get into a good college . . . I won't have a good career . . . I won't get married and I won't have children." And, she would say, "If I don't sanitize my hands after I touch something, I will get sick . . . my grades will go down . . ." and her catastrophic hypothetical life would ensue. She didn't just think this way on occasion, as many teenagers may during a freak-out moment; this was the way her mind worked throughout her day, every day. As I understand, this is common with anxiety disorders, which makes more sense now as to why Jillian sought out the calming, antianxiety experience of negative energy balance by self-starvation.

In an earlier chapter I shared how Jillian lacked decision-making skills (which went hand-in-hand with her low self-confidence). When I learned of her deficiency in this regard, I was shocked at how unaware I was that she struggled in this area and that unknowingly my responses perpetuated the problem. I sought training to encourage her to make simple daily decisions. Doing so was supportive.

FACILITATING STRATEGIES

I learned to respond in a manner to help her need less and less reassurance and develop self-confidence. This was a learning process and part of her journey as well as mine. The takeaway here is, had I not learned what she was learning or working on, I would not have been able to support her to the fullest extent possible.

When Amelia struggled (and still struggles) with thoughts about being fat or feeling fat, I remind her of the different coping skills and strategies she has learned (such as thought challenging or the use of evidence questions like "Do your clothes fit the same?" or "Do you wear the same size clothes?"). Again, learning what your loved one is learning is instrumental.

I wish I could say that my husband and I were able to use the suggestions presented in this book perfectly and that our daughters' recoveries were smooth sailing. They certainly weren't. Much of what we learned, we learned from our mistakes and were based on previous experiences. Also, I have since learned much (that I wished we had known then). We, especially I, got angry, frustrated, and even resentful. But I can say that by learning what my daughters were learning, many disagreements were prevented and our frustration with one another greatly decreased. I strongly recommend seeking information from the professionals on an ongoing basis to support the use of skills and strategies in your loved one's daily life outside of treatment. Request clarification and examples from the treatment team as needed.

Equally important as facilitating your loved one's use

of strategies is gradually reducing the reminders and cues to promote independence. As he or she is learning in recovery, provide assistance in a hierarchal manner. Initially, your loved one may need consistent supervision and assistance. Gradually, he or she will need less supervision and assistance. Be mindful to allow your loved one to grow in his or her level of independence. For example, initially the individual may need constant supervision during meals; maybe he or even needs to be fed or handed the food or drink to consume what is needed. Then, maybe he or she only needs the fork pushed closer on occasion; next it's a few verbal prompts. Eventually no assistance is needed and the individual is eating more and more on his or her own without supervision. Don't promote dependence on you; instead be aware of the progress your loved one is making toward the ultimate goal of independent eating for proper nutrition and maintaining a healthy weight.

Again, remember to take very good care of yourself. You may need support as well. Rely on family and friends for help. Seek therapy or counseling if needed. Attend family support groups if offered in your area. Follow the recommendations for self-care, maintain balance in your life, and incorporate healthy lifestyle habits yourself. You cannot be of any help if you are constantly overwhelmed and stressed. You will provide your best support if you nourish your body by eating well, resting, by getting enough sleep, and exercise.

Eating disorder specialist Carolyn Costin said it best when she proclaimed, "Recover*ed* Is a Reality!"

References

Introduction: Could This Be an Eating Disorder?

National Eating Disorders Association. "Treatment." www.nationaleatingdisorders.org/treatment

Chapter 1: Important Concepts

Baker Dennis, Amy, and Helfman, Bethany. National Eating Disorders Association.www.nationaleatingdisorders.org/substance-abuse-and-eating-disorders

Bulik, Cynthia. (2014). "Negative Energy Balance: A Biological Trap for People Prone to Anorexia Nervosa." https://uncexchanges.org/2014/12/01/negative-energy-balance-a-biological-trap-for-people-prone-to-anorexia-nervosa/

Goldhamer, Lauren. (2009). "Are eating disorders addictions?" *Moods Magazine,* Winter, 13–16.

Muhlheim, Lauren. (2016). "Anosognosia and Anorexia When a Loved One with Anorexia Does Not Believe They Are Ill." www.verywell.com/anosognosia-and-anorexia-3573545

Muhlheim, Lauren. (2015). "'Unintentional' Onset of Anorexia." http://eatingdisordertherapyla.com/unintentional-onset-of-anorexia/

National Institute of Mental Health's (NIMH) (2007). "Eating Disorders." www.nimh.nih.gov/news/science-news/2007/study-tracks-prevalence-of-eating-disorders.shtml

O'Tool, Julie, M.D. (2015). "Avoiding Negative Energy Balance." www.kartiniclinic.com/blog/post/avoiding-negative-energy-balance

Quittner, Ella. (2011). "Are Eating Disorders a Form of Substance Abuse? The overwhelming urges of people with bulimia or binge eating disorder look a lot like alcoholism or drug addiction, experts say." www.health.com/health/article/0,, 20538012, 00.html

Ross, Carolyn. (2012). *Psychology Today*. "Eight Surprising Parallels Between Food and Drug Addictions." www.psychologytoday.com/blog/real-healing/201209/eight-surprising-parallels-between-food-and-drug-addictions

Chapter 2 Eating Disorder Basics

Arcelus, J., Mitchell, A. J., Wales, J., and Nielsen, S. (2011). "Mortality Rates In Patients with Anorexia Nervosa and Other Eating Disorders." *Archives of General Psychiatry*, 68(7), 724–731.

Bulik, Cynthia. (2014). "Negative Energy Balance: A Biological Trap for People Prone to Anorexia Nervosa." https://uncexchanges.org/2014/12/01/negative-energy-balance-a-biological-trap-for-people-prone-to-anorexia-nervosa/

Gearhardt, Ashley (2011). "Binge Eating Disorder and Food Addiction." www.ncbi.nlm.nih.gov/pmc/articles/PMC3671377/

Insel, Thomas, M.D. (NIMH), 2009, www.youtube.com/watch?v=wu6QaR_gO9I

Muhlheim, Lauren. (2015). "'Unintentional' Onset of Anorexia." http://eatingdisordertherapyla.com/unintentional-onset-of-anorexia/

National Association of Anorexia Nervosa and Associated Disorders. www.anad.org/get-information/about-eating-disorders/eating-disorders-statistics/

References

National Institute of Mental Health's (NIMH) guide. (2011). *Eating Disorders: Facts About Eating Disorders and the Search for Solutions*, NIH Publication No 01-4901. www.nimh.nih.gov/health/publica tions/eating-disorders-new-trifold/eating-disorders-pdf_148810.pdf

O'Tool, Julie, M.D. (2015). "Avoiding Negative Energy Balance." www.kartiniclinic.com/blog/post/avoiding-negative-energy-balance

Quittner, Ella. (2011). "Are Eating Disorders a Form of Substance Abuse? The Overwhelming Urges of People with Bulimia or Binge Eating Disorder Look a Lot Like Alcoholism or Drug Addiction, Experts Say." www.health.com/health/article/0,,20538012, 00.html

The Renfrew Center Foundation for Eating Disorders. (2003). "Eating Disorders: 101 Guide: A Summary of Issues, Statistics, and Resources." www.renfrew.org.

Substance Abuse and Mental Health Services Administration (SAMHSA), The Center for Mental Health Services (CCMHS), Offices of the U.S. Department Health and Human Services. "Eating Disorder Statistics." https://www.ndsu.edu/fileadmin/counseling/Eating _Disorder_Statistics.pdf

Chapter 3: Why Is This Happening?

Baker, Jessica, Ph.D. (2015). "Causes of Eating Disorders." www.mirror -mirror.org/causes-of-eating-disorders.htm

Baker, Jessica, Ph.D. (2015). "The Genetic Risk for Eating Disorders and the Anorexia Nervosa Genetics Initiative (ANGI)." www.mirror -mirror.org/genetics-and-eating-disorders.htm

Bulik, Cynthia. (2014). "Negative Energy Balance: A Biological Trap for People Prone to Anorexia Nervosa." https://uncexchanges .org/2014/12/01/negative-energy-balance-a-biological-trap-for -people-prone-to-anorexia-nervosa/

Centers for Disease Control and Prevention (CDC): National Center for Health Statistics Center. (2012). "Body Measurements." www.cdc.gov/nchs/fastats/body-measurements.htm

Christine, R. (2014). "The Average Woman vs. The Average Model, Thoughtful Woman." www.thoughtfulwomen.org/2014/03/19/average-woman-vs-average-model/

LeGrange, D., Lock, J., Loeb, K., and Nicholls, D. (2009). "Academy of Eating Disorders Position Paper: The Role of the Family in Eating Disorders." www.aedweb.org/downloads/Role_of_Family.pdf

National Institute of Mental Health's (NIMH) guide. (2011). *Eating Disorders: Facts About Eating Disorders and the Search for Solutions.* NIH Publication No 01-4901.

Striegel-Moore, R., and Bulik, C. (2007). *Risk Factors for Eating Disorders.* American Psychologist, 62(3), 181–198.

Chapter 4: The Enigmatic Aspects of a Mysterious Disease

Baker, Jessica, Ph.D. (2015). "Causes of Eating Disorders." www.mirror-mirror.org/causes-of-eating-disorders.htm

Ravin, S. (May 2015). "After Weight Restoration: The Role of Motivation." www.blog.drsarahravin.com/eating-disorders/after-weight-restoration-the-role-of-motivation/

Sim LA. (2014). "Family-Based Therapy for Anorexia Nervosa in Adolescents." Medical Professional Video Center. Mayo Clinic. www.mayoclinic.org/medical-professionals/clinical-updates/psychiatry-psychologyfamily-based-therapy-highly-effective-for-most-anorexia-patients

Chapter 5: Getting Clear on Distorted Body Image

Eating Disorder Hope. "How Body Image Relates to Eating Disorders." www.eatingdisorderhope.com/information/body-image/how-body-image-relates-to-eating-disorders

Keizer, Anouk, et al. (2013). "Too Fat to Fit Through the Door:

References

First Evidence for Disturbed Body-Scaled Action in Anorexia Nervosa During Locomotion." http://journals.plos.org/plosone/article?id=10.1371/journal.pone.0064602

NEDA. "What Is body image?" www.nationaleatingdisorders.org/what-body-image

Seeger, G., Braus, D. F., Ruf, M., Golderger, U., and Schmidt, M. H. (2002). "Body Image Distortion Reveals Amygdala Activation in Patients with Anorexia-Nervosa—A Functional Magnetic Resonance Imaging Study." *Neuroscience Letters*, 326(1), 25–28. DOI 10.1016/S0304-3940(02)00312-

Wagner, A., Ruf, M., Braus, D. F., and Schmidt, M. H. (2003). "Neuronal Activity Changes and Body Image Distortion in Anorexia Nervosa." *Neuroreport*, 14(17), 2193–2197.

Chapter 6: The Eating Disordered Mind and Change in Personality

Bryant-Waugh, R., and Lask, B. *Eating Disorders: A Parent's Guide Revised Edition*, New York, NY: Routledge, 2004.

Chapter 7: How to Talk About Treatment

NEDA. (2015). "NEDA TOOLKIT for Parents." Retrieved from www.nationaleatingdisorders.org/sites/default/files/Toolkits/Parent Toolkit.pdf

Chapter 8: Treatment Options

Farrar, T. (2014). "Eating Disorders Eating Disorder Statistics." www.mirror-mirror.org/eating-disorders-statistics.htm

Maudsleyparents.org. "Maudsley Misconceptions." www.maudsleyparents.org/maudsleymisconceptions.html

Maudsleyparents.org. "What is Maudsley?" www.maudsleyparents.org/whatismaudsley.html

Muhlheim, L. (2015). "Cognitive Behavioral Therapy." www.eatingdisordertherapyla.com/about-us/our-psychotherapy-treatment-philosophy/cognitive-behavioral-therapy/

Muhlheim, Lauren. (2016). "Meal Support in the Treatment of Eating Disorders: How Meal Support Can Help Eating Disorder Recovery." www.verywell.com/meal-support-in-the-treatment-of-eating-disorders-1138365

NEDA. (2015). "NEDA TOOLKIT for Parents." Retrieved from www.nationaleatingdisorders.org/sites/default/files/Toolkits/Parent Toolkit.pdf

Strober, M., Freeman, R., Morrell, W. (1997). "The Long-Term Course of Severe Anorexia Nervosa in Adolescents: Survival Analysis of Recovery, Relapse, and Outcome Predictors over 10–15 Years in a Progressive Study." *International Journal of Eating Disorders*, 22(4), 339–360. www.ncbi.nlm.nih.gov/pubmed/9356884

Chapter 11: Facilitating Strategies

National Eating Disorders Association. "Treatment." www.nationaleatingdisorders.org/treatment

About the Author

Caroline R. Blaire is a speech therapist in practice for more than twenty-five years. With her two daughters now recovered and living full, independent lives, Caroline happily empty nests with her husband in Wisconsin.

www.ingramcontent.com/pod-product-compliance
Lightning Source LLC
Chambersburg PA
CBHW051653040426
42446CB00009B/1108